The Key of the Kingdom

The Key of the Kingdom

A Book of Stories and Poems
for Children

COLLECTED BY

ELISABETH GMEYNER AND JOYCE RUSSELL

Bell Pond Books

2004

Publisher's Note

The Key of the Kingdom, was first published in England in 1951. Much-loved by earlier generations, it is something of a Waldorf classic. Based on the first (1928) reader of the Stuttgart Waldorf School in Germany, it was intended to "be a friend and companion" to children in "their early schooldays." As these quotations indicate, however, although having perennial value, charm, and humor, and demonstrating a joyous love of language, *The Key of the Kingdom* is also very much of its own time and place. This means that many of the pieces originally written by their authors in English still contain the universal "Man" and "he." We felt justified in changing such language when it occurred in translated pieces, but we felt that we had no right to change those written in English. Thus, although it is our editorial policy to use gender universal language, they stand here as written. We feel that this is a marvelous collection, well worth reissuing. It is full of imagination, fantasy, and wit—in the spirit of George MacDonald and C.S. Lewis—and still well-suited to lead children to a love of the world and the word. We hope twenty-first century parents and children think so too!

From a book first published by Rudolf Steiner Press, London, in 1951.
This edition copyright Bell Pond Books, Inc.

Bell Pond Books, 400 Main Street, Great Barrington, MA 01230

www.bellpondbooks.com

10 9 8 7 6 5 4 3 2 1

Printed in the United States of America

Contents

This Is the Key of the Kingdom	Anonymous, English	9
Pleasure It Is	William Cornish	10
Mother Earth	Eileen Hutchins	11
The Fir and the Larch	Eileen Hutchins	12
The Birch and the Poplar	Legend	13
When Mary Goes Walking	Patrick Chalmers	13
St. Peter and the Goat	Legend	14
The Rose and the Lily	Eileen Hutchins	14
In May I Go A-walking	Folk Song	15
The Light of the Sun	Rudolf Steiner	15
The Birds	Samuel Taylor Coleridge	16
The Magpie and Her Children	Brothers Grimm	17
The Sheepdog	Fable	17
The Stag, the Hare and the Donkey	Fable	18
The Eagle (fable)	Lessing	18
The Eagle	Alfred Lord Tennyson	18
The Town Mouse & the Country Mouse	Fable	19
He and She	Anon	20
Silver	Walter de la Mare	21
Night Piece	Robert Herrick	21
By the Moon	Thomas Ravenscroft	22
The Goblin Workman	English Folk Tale	23
Lazy Jack	English Folk Tale	25
Jog On	William Shakespeare	26
Nicholas Nye	Walter de la Mare	27
The Miller, His Son and Their Ass	Fable	29
Come a Riddle	Riddle	30
In Marble Walls	Riddle	30
My Beak is Below	Riddle	30
The Wind and the Sun	Fable	31
Cows	P.S. Moffat	31

I Will Go with My Father A-Ploughing	*Seosamh Maccathmhaoil*	32
The Blossoms of the Heather	*Legend*	33
The Brook	*Alfred Lord Tennyson*	34
Come Unto These Yellow Sands	*William Shakespeare*	35
Hie Away!	*Sir Walter Scott*	36
Full Fathom Five	*William Shakespeare*	36
The Seal Woman	*Scottish Folk Tale*	37
Cap O' Rushes	*English Folk Tale*	38
The Night	*William Blake*	39
Matthew, Mark, Luke and John	*Old Rhyme*	42
The Twelve Apostles	*Brothers Grimm*	43
The Christmas Rose	*Caroline Von Heydebrand*	44
The Sun Is in My Heart	*A. C. Harwood*	45
Mary on the Flight into Egypt	*Legend*	46
When Icicles Hang by the Wall	*William Shakespeare*	47
The Three Sillies	*English Folk Tale*	48
The Wise Men of Gotham	*English Folk Tale*	50
Jack the Cunning Thief	*Irish Folk Tale*	52
How A Little Flower Got Its Name	*Legend*	55
The Violet	*After Rudolf Steiner*	56
Pippa's Song	*Robert Browning*	57
The Shepherd's Sweet Lot	*William Blake*	57
Lines Written in March	*William Wordsworth*	58
The Lamb	*William Blake*	59
The Echoing Green	*William Blake*	60
Spring, the Sweet Spring	*Thomas Nash*	61
A Grace	*Rudolf Steiner*	61
St. Kevin and the Blackbird	*Legend*	62
The Robin's Song	*Old English rhyme*	63
St. Francis Bids the Swallows Be Silent	*Story*	64
St. Francis Preaches to the Birds	*Story*	64
St. Francis and the Wolf of Gubbio	*Story*	65
Canticle to the Sun	*Transcribed by Lawrence Edwards*	67
The Larks at the Death of St. Francis	*Story*	68
The Skylark	*Elisabeth Gmeyner*	68

Laughing Song	*William Blake*	69
Over Hill Over Dale	*William Shakespeare*	69
Where the Bee Sucks	*William Shakespeare*	70
You Spotted Snakes	*William Shakespeare*	70
Lusmore at Knockgrafton	*Irish Folk Tale*	71
When Cats Run Home	*Alfred Lord Tennyson*	74
Meg Merrilies	*John Keats*	75
Beauty and the Beast	*French Fairy Tale*	76
The Crystal Ball	*Brother Grimm*	78
The Cedar	*Wolfgang von Goethe*	80
Michaelmas Song	*A.C. Harwood*	81
Michael the Victorious	*Old Gaelic*	82
St. George	*From the Golden Legend*	82
The Ride-by-Nights	*Walter de la Mare*	83
November	*Elisabeth Gmeyner*	84
The Ploughman's Charm	*Old English*	85
Our Lord and the Poor Man	*Russian Legend*	85
St. Columba and the White Horse	*Legend*	87
The Rune of St. Patrick	*Old Gaelic*	88
Gaelic Rune of Hospitality	*Old Gaelic*	88
When Days Are Darkest	*P. S. Moffat*	89
Christ and St. Nicholas	*Russian Legend*	89
St. Christopher	*Legend*	92
Mary's Journey through the Stars	*After Karl Schubert*	94
The Legend of St. Bridget	*Legend*	95
The Date Palm	*From an Apocryphal Gospel*	98
When Joseph Was A-Walking	*Carol*	99
I sing of a Maiden	*Carol*	100
New Year Carol	*Old English*	101
The Ball of Crystal & the Saucer of Silver	*Russian Fairy Tale*	102
Bashtchelik	*Serbian Fairy Tale*	107
Alleluia for All Things	*A.C. Harwood*	124
Morning Prayer	*Rudolf Steiner*	125
To the Grown Ups		126
Acknowledgments		126

This is the Key

This is the Key of the Kingdom:
In that Kingdom is a city;
In that city is a town;
In that town there is a street;
In that street there winds a lane;
In that lane there is a yard;
In that yard there is a house;
In that house there waits a room;
In that room an empty bed;
And on that bed a basket—
A Basket of Sweet Flowers;
　　Of Flowers, of Flowers;
　　A Basket of Sweet Flowers.

Flowers in a Basket;
Basket on the bed;
Bed in the chamber;
Chamber in the house;
House in the weedy yard;
Yard in the winding lane;
Lane in the broad street;
Street in the high town;
Town in the city;
City in the Kingdom—
This is the Key of the Kingdom.
　　Of the Kingdom this is the Key.

　　　　　　—Anonymous, English

9

Pleasure It Is

Pleasure it is
To hear I wis
The birdes sing,
The deer in the dale,
The sheep in the vale,
The corn springing;
God's purveyance
For sustenance
It is for man.
Then we always
To Him give praise
And thank Him then
And thank Him then.

—*William Cornish*

Mother Earth

Mother Earth,
Mother Earth,
Take our seed
And give it birth.

Father Sun,
Gleam and glow
Until the roots
Begin to grow.

Sister Rain
Sister Rain
Shed thy tears
To swell the grain.

Brother Wind
Breathe and blow
Then the blade
Green will grow.

Earth and Sun
And Wind and Rain
Turn to gold
The living grain.

—*Eileen Hutchins*

The Fir and the Larch

NCE OUR LORD was passing through the woods when the rain began to fall. First there were gentle little drops, then a heavy down-pour, and at last hailstones as large as nuts came rattling through the trees. Our Lord sought shelter under the wide branches, but most of the trees shivered in the cold so that the hailstones beat upon Him and the drops were shaken down from every side. At last He stood under the Fir tree, and the Fir held herself erect and spread out her arms to protect Him so that not a drop could pierce her branches. Then our Lord blessed the Fir tree so that in summer and winter her boughs are always green.

Near the Fir tree stood her little sister the Larch. She had trembled with pride and pleasure when our Lord passed by, so that she had thoughtlessly shaken the rain from her boughs. In the winter her branches were bare, and she looked with envy at the green Fir tree. But soon all the trees in the forest were robed in mantles of snow and their bare naked trunks were hidden from the sun and the stars.

It was early in the spring and the snow still covered the ground when there went a murmur through the trees that our Lord was passing by. All were glad to meet Him in their white shining robes. Just then a flock of birds flew by, crying and calling to one another for they could find no place to rest their wings among the canopies of snow. The Larch pitied the birds who had nowhere to rest and she shook her boughs until they were bare so that the birds could alight among the branches.

Then our Lord passed by and the Larch tried to hide her nakedness behind the other trees. But our Lord came to her and said: "You have sheltered and loved the birds and so every spring your branches will be the greenest of all the trees that bear needles. And wherever the birds have rested you shall bear beautiful pink cones in memory of your love for them."

And that is why in the spring the Larch bears such beautiful little pink cones.

—*Eileen Hutchins*

The Birch and the Poplar

S THE LORD JESUS was going on his way, He saw two trees growing near a pond. When one of them noticed the Lord, it began to bow with joy and to bend its branches to greet Him. This was the Birch. The Poplar, however, did not even move, though Jesus passed close by. He therefore granted to the Birch light airy branches, which it can bend to the earth with every breath of wind, as if it wanted to greet someone. The Poplar stands firm like a tower, lifting its head haughtily to the clouds.

—Legend

When Mary Goes Walking

When Mary goes walking
The autumn winds blow
The poplars they curtsey
The larches bend low,
The oaks and the beeches
Their gold they fling down
To make her a carpet
To make her a crown.

—Patrick Chalmers

St. Peter and the Goat

HEN CHRIST was still walking on the earth with His disciples, Peter was astonished that such strange things were happening in the world and that his Master did not seem to mind about them. Thereupon Jesus handed him His staff as a sign that from now onwards He gave the ruling of the world into Peter's hands.

Peter began to rule. After a while there came a poor woman driving her goat out to pasture; she commended it to God's care as she herself had to go back to the village to look after her children.

Following his Master's wish, Peter took the wayward little creature into his care and leaped after it uphill and down dale and through bushes and hedges. You can well imagine how the old man sweated and how glad he was when he got the goat safely back to the woman's house in the evening.

When our Lord asked him if he wanted to rule any longer, Peter said humbly, "No, Lord, I have found out that I have not even enough wisdom to rule a goat, how little then, am I able to rule the world! "

—Legend

The Rose and the Lily

HE DEVIL ONCE came to God and said: "Let us see who can make the most beautiful flower."

God created a shining white lily, but the Devil could only make hard, sharp thorns. Then the Devil said: "Let us give one another the plants we have made." So God took the thorns and blessed them saying: "Strive to reach the light." And lo and behold! From the dark wood, there bloomed the most beautiful red roses.

The Devil drew near the white lily to carry it away to his home underground but it shone so brightly that he dared not touch it and the little devils, looking out, began to scream: "Do not bring it here, we cannot bear it."

And so to-day the Rose and the Lily grow side by side in the light of the sun.

— Eileen Hutchins

In May I Go A-Walking

In May I go a-walking
To hear the linnet sing,
The blackbird and the throstle
A-praising God the King.

It cheers the heart to hear them
To see the leaves unfold
The meadows covered over
With buttercups of gold.

— Folk Song

The Light of the Sun

The light of the sun is flooding
The breadths of space,
The song of the birds is sounding
Through realms of air,
The wakening plants are springing
From depths of earth,
And filled with thanks the souls of men are risi
To spirits of the world.

— Rudolf Steiner

The Birds

Do you ask what the birds say?
The sparrow, the dove,
The linnet, the thrush say:
I love and I love.

In winter they're silent,
The wind is so strong;
What it says I don't know,
But it sings a loud song.

But green leaves and blossoms
And sunny warm weather
And singing and loving,
All come back together.

Then the lark is so brimful
Of gladness and love,
The green fields below him,
The blue sky above,

That he sings and he sings
And forever sings he:
I love my love
And my love loves me.

—*Samuel Taylor Coleridge*

The Magpie and Her Children

 MAGPIE led her children out into the fields so that they might learn to find their own food. They did not like it and would rather have returned to their nest and let their mother bring them food in her beak, which was far less trouble.

"My children," she said, "you are big enough to feed yourselves. My mother sent me out much earlier."

"But the archers will kill us," answered the children.

"No, no," said the mother, "they need time to aim; if you see them raising their bows, then fly away."

"We will," said the children, "but what if one of them picks up a stone and throws it at us, no aiming is needed for that. What then?"

"But you can easily see," said the mother, "how he bends down to pick up a stone."

"But supposing he was carrying a stone in his hand all the time and was ready to throw it at any minute?"

"Oh, what a lot you know!" the mother said, and she flew away and left them to themselves.

—Brothers Grimm

The Sheepdog

O NE EVENING an old sheepdog, the faithful guardian of his master's sheep, was on his way home. Little lapdogs yapped at him in the street. He trotted on without looking round. When he came to the meat stall, a butcher's dog asked him how he could bear such continual barking and why he did not take one of them by the scruff of his neck.

"No," answered the sheepdog, "they do not worry or bite me. I must keep my teeth for wolves."

—Fable

The Stag, the Hare and the Donkey

HERE WAS ONCE a stag with beautiful antlers walking across the fields. A hare ran past and when he saw him, stopped in amazement. Then, getting on his hind legs, he approached the stag, saying, "Look at me! I am a little stag, for if I stretch my ears, they are like your antlers."

A donkey heard this and said: "You are right, we are all of one family."

The stag cast a side glance at them and went back to his woods.

—Fable

The Eagle

HY DO you rear your young ones so high up in the air?" a man asked the eagle. The eagle answered, "If I reared them down on the earth, how would they venture so near the sun when they are older?"

—Lessing

The Eagle

He clasps the crag with crooked hands;
Close to the sun in lonely lands,
Ringed with the azure world, he stands.
The wrinkled sea beneath him crawls;
He watches from his mountain walls,
And like a thunderbolt he falls.

—Alfred Lord Tennyson

The Town Mouse and the Country Mouse

THE TOWN MOUSE went to visit a country mouse, who fed her on acorns, nuts, seeds and whatever she could find; but the town mouse said: "This is poor fare. Come with me, I will find enough dainties for both of us." The country mouse agreed and they set out together for the town. When they arrived, they went straight to the larder of a big house; here they found bread, meat, bacon, sausages, cheese and whatever a mouse could wish for.

The town mouse said: "Now eat and be of good cheer, such dishes I have every day in plenty."

Suddenly they heard a clattering of keys, the cook was at the door! The mice were frightened and ran away. The town mouse soon found her hole but the country mouse did not know where to go; she ran along the wall to and fro and barely escaped with her life.

When the cook had gone, the town mouse said: "Now we will enjoy ourselves; there is no more danger."

But the country mouse answered: "It is all very well for you to say this, you knew where to hide, but I nearly died of fear. You can stay here in a rich town house and eat your sausages and bacon. I will remain a poor country mouse and eat my acorns. You are never safe from the cook, the cat, the traps; the whole house is your enemy. I want to be back at home, safe and free in my little hole in the fields."

—Fable

He and She

He was a rat and she was a rat,
And down in one hole they did dwell,
And both were as black as a witch's cat
And they loved one another well.

He had a tail and she had a tail,
Both long and curling and fine;
And each said: "Yours is the finest tail
In the world excepting mine."

He smelt the cheese and she smelt the cheese,
And they both pronounced it good;
And both remarked it would greatly add
To the charms of their daily food.

So he ventured out and she ventured out
And I saw them go with pain;
But what befell them I never can tell,
For they never came back again.

—Anon

Silver

Slowly, silently, now the moon
Walks the night in her silver shoon.
This way and that she peers and sees
Silver fruit upon silver trees.
One by one the casements catch
Her beams beneath the silvery thatch.
Couched in his kennel like a log
With paws of silver sleeps the dog;
From their shadowy cotes the white breasts peep
Of doves in a silver feathered sleep;
A harvest mouse goes scampering by,
With silver claws and silver eye;
And moveless fish in the water gleam
By silver reeds in a silver stream.

—*Walter de la Mare*

Night Piece

Her eyes the glow worm lend thee,
The shooting stars attend thee,
And the elves also,
Whose little eyes glow
Like sparks of fire, befriend thee.

No will-o'-the-wisp mislight thee
Nor snake or slow worm bite thee
But on, on thy way
Not making a stay
Since ghost there's none to affright thee.

Let not the dark thee cumber,
What though the moon does slumber?
The stars of the night
Will lend thee their light
Like tapers clear without number.

—*Robert Herrick*

By the Moon

By the moon we sport and play
With the night begins our day;
As we dance the dew doth fall
Trip it little urchins all;
Lightly as the little bee,
Two by two and three by three;
And about go we, and about go we.

"I do come about the copse
Leaping upon flower tops,
Then I get upon a fly
She carries me above the sky
And trip and go."

"When a dewdrop falleth down
And doth light upon my crown
Then I shake my head and skip
And about I trip.
Two by two and three by three
And about go we and about go we."

—*Thomas Ravenscroft*

The Goblin Workman

N A WILD MOORLAND VALE in Yorkshire, there once lived a poor farmer. He worked hard from morning till night, but had much ado to make ends meet and if the harvest was poor, things went badly with him. One night, as he lay in bed, thinking over his troubles, he heard the sound of a flail coming from a nearby barn. Soon his wife was awakened by the thumping, but neither of them dared to go and look as they were sure it could be no mortal working at such an hour. In the morning, they plucked up their courage and went to the barn. What was their surprise to find the corn lying there piled up to the rafters, more than a strong man could thresh in a week. The farmer was delighted. "Wife," he said, "it must be a goblin; I will leave more corn ready to be threshed to-night."

This he did and sure enough, in the morning there was again a great pile of corn ready threshed, standing in the barn and so it happened on the following nights until all the harvest was finished. After this the goblin would do other work so that soon the farmer grew rich and prosperous. When haymaking or harvesting time came round, he had no need to hire extra help, the goblin did it all and the farmer slept peacefully in his bed at night, knowing that everything would be done for him. At last he said to his wife, "Wife, I think we should reward our helper who has served us so well. Let us put out a bowl of cream and a cake for him tonight."

"Willingly," replied his wife and that evening they carried a bowl of thick rich cream and a cake hot from the oven, out to the barn. In the morning, plate and bowl were empty and the work had been done as usual. The farmer was glad to think that he had been able to make some slight return for the goblin's service, and they put out food and drink every night.

So things went on for some years and the farmer and his wife lived in great prosperity. But, as the wife grew richer, she became miserly and began to think that it was a waste of good food to give the best cakes and cream to a goblin.

"He will not know the difference," she said to herself, and that night she put a stale loaf and a bowl of skim milk in the barn. Next morning no work had been done by the goblin and after that he did no more. No longer would he bring in the hay or the corn and never again was the sound of his flail heard in the night. The farmer and his wife put all the dainties they could think of in the barn, but nothing appeased the goblin, and worse befell, as he turned his attention to mischief and did all he could to plague them, particularly the wife, whose meanness he resented. If it was her day for churning, turn as she would, the butter would not come; if she made cheeses, they turned out badly; the goblin would also let out the chickens so that the fox got them. Then on cold nights he would pull the bedclothes off the farmer and his wife when they were snug in bed, and rattle all the pots and pans until no one had any rest.

At last the farmer lost patience. "We cannot stay here," he said, "Our lives have become a burden to us. I have lived in this house all my days, but the time has come to leave."

The wife sorrowfully agreed and they piled up all their household belongings on one of the farm carts, climbed up themselves and set out to find a new home. As they jolted slowly along the road, they met an old man whom they had known for many years.

"What, old friend! "he cried, "Are you flitting?"

Before the farmer had time to reply, a deep hollow voice sounded from the top of the cart, "Yes, we're flitting!"

The goblin had come too! "Well," said the farmer, "if you are flitting with us, we'll flit home again," and he turned the horses round and returned to his old farm.

Now whether this last trick satisfied the goblin or whether he decided to live elsewhere, no one ever knew, but certain it is that the farmer and his wife heard no more of him and lived in peace for the rest of their lives.

—English Folk Tale

Lazy Jack

ONCE UPON A TIME, there was a boy whose name was Jack and he lived with his mother on a common. The common was bare and dreary and they were very poor; Jack's mother got her living by spinning but Jack was so lazy that he would do nothing but sit in the sun in the summer and in the chimney corner in winter. So he earned the name of Lazy Jack. At last his mother got tired of seeing him so idle and said that if he did not begin to work for his living she would turn him out of doors to get along as best he could.

Thereupon Jack went and hired himself to a farmer who lived nearby; the farmer gave him a penny for his wages but he had never had any money of his own before, and as he was coming home he lost it crossing over a brook. When he told this to his mother she said, "You silly fellow, you should have put it in your pocket."

"I will next time," said Jack.

Next day Jack hired himself to a cowkeeper who gave him a jar of milk for his day's work. Mindful of his mother's words, Jack put the jar into the large pocket of his coat and set off home spilling the milk with every step till not a drop remained.

"You silly fellow," cried his mother, "you should have carried it on your head." "I'll do so next time," said Jack.

Next day Jack hired himself again to a farmer who promised to give him a cream cheese as wages. At the end of the day, Jack set off home with the cheese on his head, but when he got there it was completely spoilt, part having melted and part being matted with his hair.

"You silly fellow," said his mother, "you should have carried it carefully in your hands."

"I'll do so next time," said Jack.

The following day Jack went out and hired himself to a baker who gave him a large tom cat for his day's work. Jack took puss and set off for home carrying him very carefully in his hands but after a bit the cat scratched so hard that Jack was forced to let him go.

When his mother heard this, "You silly fellow," she said, "you should have tied a string round it and pulled it along behind you."

"I'll do so next time," said Jack.

Next day Jack hired himself to a butcher, who gave him a leg of mutton for his pains. Jack took the mutton, tied a string round it and dragged it home through the dirt. When he got there the meat was quite spoilt. His mother lost her temper with him, for the next day was Sunday and now there would be nothing but cabbage for dinner.

"You silly fellow," she cried, "you should have carried it on your shoulder."
"I'll do so another time," said Jack.

On the Monday Jack went out once more and hired himself to a cattle keeper, who rewarded him with a donkey. Jack thought of his mother's words and tried to hoist the donkey on to his shoulders, but although he was strong, he found it a very difficult task. At last he succeeded and set off walking slowly along the road.

Now on his way, he passed by the house of a rich man, who had only one daughter; she was very beautiful but deaf and dumb. The doctors said she would never speak until someone made her laugh and her father promised her hand in marriage to anyone who could do so. This young lady happened to be looking out of the window and saw Jack passing by, carrying his donkey on his shoulders with its legs sticking up in the air. The sight was so comical that she burst out laughing and was at once able to hear and speak. Her father was delighted and fulfilled his promise by marrying her to Jack, who thus became a fine gentleman. They lived in a large house and Jack's mother lived with them in great happiness till she died.

—*English Folk Tale*

Jog On

Jog on, jog on, the footpath way
And merrily hent the stile-a
Your merry heart goes all the way
Your sad tires in a mile-a.

—*William Shakespeare*

Nicholas Nye

Thistle and darnel and dock grew there,
And a bush, in the corner, of May,
On the orchard wall I used to sprawl,
In the blazing heat of the day;
Half asleep and half awake,
While the birds went twittering by,
And nobody there my lone to share
But Nicholas Nye.

Nicholas Nye was lean and grey
Lame of a leg and old;
More than a score of donkey's years
He had seen since he was foaled.
He munched the thistles, purple and spiked,
Would sometimes stoop and sigh
And turn his head as if he said
"Poor Nicholas Nye! "

Alone with his shadows he'd drowse in the meadow,
Lazily swinging his tail,
At break of day he used to bray-—
Not much too hearty and hale;
But a wonderful gumption was under his skin,
And a clear calm light in his eye,
And once in a while he'd smile-—
Would Nicholas Nye.

Seem to be smiling at me, he would,
From his bush, in the corner, of May—
Bony and ownerless, widowed and worn,
Knobble-kneed, lonely and grey;
And over the grass would seem to pass
'Neath the deep dark blue of the sky,
Something much better than words between me
And Nicholas Nye.

But dusk would come in the apple boughs,
The green of the glow-worm shine,
The birds in nest would crouch to rest,
And home I'd trudge to mine;
And there, in the moonlight, dark with dew,
Asking not wherefore nor why,
Would brood like a ghost, and as still as a post
Old Nicholas Nye.

—Walter de la Mare

28

The Miller, His Son and Their Ass

 MILLER AND HIS SON were driving their ass to a neighboring fair to sell him. They had not gone far when they met with a troop of girls returning from the town, talking and laughing. "Look there! "cried one of them, "did you ever see such fools, to be trudging along the road on foot, when they might be riding!" The miller, hearing this, bade his son get on the ass and walked along by the side of him.

Presently they came to a group of old men, earnestly talking together. "There!" said one of them, "it proves what I was saying. What respect is shown to old age in these days? Do you see that idle young rogue riding, while his old father has to walk? Get down, you young scrapegrace! and let the old man rest his weary limbs." Upon this, the father made his son dismount, and got up himself.

In this manner they had not gone far when they met a company of women and children. "Why, you lazy old fellow," cried several tongues at once, "how can you ride upon the beast, while that poor little lad there can hardly keep pace by the side of you." The good-natured miller immediately took up his son behind him.

They had now almost reached the town. "Pray, honest friend," said a townsman, "is that ass your own?" "Yes," said the old man. "Oh! One would not have thought so," said the other, "by the way you load him. Why, you two fellows are better able to carry the poor beast than he you!" "Anything to please you," said the old man. "We can but try." So, both getting down, they tied the ass's legs together, and by the help of a pole, began to carry him on their shoulders over a bridge that led to the town. This was so comical a sight that the people ran in crowds to laugh at it; till the ass, not liking the noise or being carried upside down, kicked so hard that his cords broke and, tumbling off the pole, he fell into the river. Upon this, the old man, vexed and ashamed, made the best of his way home again.

By trying to please everybody, he had pleased nobody and lost his ass into the bargain.

—Fable

Riddles

1

Come a riddle, come a riddle,
Come a rot-tot-tot.
A wee, wee man, in a red, red coat,
A staff in his hand, and a bone in his throat,
Come a riddle, come a riddle
Come a rot-tot-tot.

2

In marble walls as white as milk
Lined with a skin as soft as silk
Within a fountain crystal clear
A golden apple doth appear.
No doors there are to this stronghold
Yet thieves break in and steal the gold.

3

My beak is below, I burrow and nose
Under the ground. I go as I'm guided
By my master the farmer, old foe of the forest;
Bent and bowed at my back he walks,
Forward pushing me over the field;
Sows on my path where I've passed along.
I came from the wood, a wagon carried me;

I was fitted with skill, I am full of wonders.
As grubbing I go, there's green on one side,
But black on the other my path is seen.
A curious prong pierces my back;
Beneath me in front, another grows down,
And forward pointing is fixed to my head.
I tear and gash the ground with my teeth
If my master steer me with skill from behind.

1. Cherry   2. Egg   3. plough

30

The Wind and the Sun

THE WIND AND THE SUN wanted to find out which of them was the stronger. Each believed himself to be more powerful than the other. While they were talking, they saw a traveller clad in a grey cloak coming along the road. "Let us see," said the wind, "which of us can make this traveller take off his cloak. He shall be acknowledged the more powerful."

The sun agreed.

Instantly the wind began to blow. He blew with all his might trying to tear off the man's cloak; but the harder he stormed, the more closely the man drew his cloak around him. The wind could not get it off.

Now it was the sun's turn.

He shone with great strength. As it grew hotter and hotter, the man unfastened his cloak; then he threw it back, and at last took it off.

The sun had won!

—Fable

Cows

Now the gentle cows are standing
Knee-deep in the dewy grass.
Dawn has found them, patient shadows,
Watching hours that softly pass.

Moving slowly over meadows,
Munching quiet unhurried ways,
They have nought to do but wander
Down the rich unheeded days.

Yet they bring about a wonder
Such as not the wisest can,
Changing common meadow grasses
Into richest food of man.

As they lie unmindful, chewing,
By a faintly sounding stream,
What new marvels are they viewing?
What deep secrets do they dream?

—P. S. Moffat

31

I Will Go with My Father A-Ploughing

I will go with my father a-ploughing
To the green field by the sea,
And the rooks and the crows and the seagulls
Will come flocking after me.
I will sing to the patient horses
With the lark in the white of the air,
And my father will sing the plough song
That blesses the cleaving share.

I will go with my father a-sowing
To the red field by the sea,
And the rooks and the gulls and the starlings
Will come flocking after me.
I will sing to the striding sowers
With the finch on the flowering sloe,
And my father will sing the seed song
That only the wise men know.

I will go with my father a-reaping
To the brown field by the sea,
And the geese and the crows and the children
Will come flocking after me.
I will sing to the weary reapers
With the wren in the heat of the sun,
And my father will sing the scythe song
That joys for the harvest done.

—*Seosamh Maccathmhaoil*

The Blossoms of the Heather

ONLY A LITTLE WHILE after the earth was made, the trees and plants came to live on it. They were happy and contented. The lily was glad because her flowers were white, the rose was glad because her flowers were red. The violet was happy because, however shyly she might hide herself away, someone would come to look for her and praise her fragrance. The daisy was happiest of all because every child in the world loved her.

The trees and plants chose homes for themselves. The oak said: "I will live in the broad fields and by the roads, and travellers may sit in my shadow." "I shall be glad to live on the waters of the pond," said the water lily. "And I shall be happy in the sunny fields," said the daisy. "My fragrance shall rise from beside some mossy stone," said the violet. Each plant chose its home.

There was one little plant, however, that had not said a word, and had not chosen a home. This was the heather. She had not the sweet fragrance of the violet and the children did not love her as they do the daisy. No blossoms had been given to her and she was too shy to ask for any. "I wish there was someone who would be glad to see me," she said.

One day, she heard the mountain say, "Dear plants, will you not come to my rocks and cover them with your brightness and beauty? In the winter they are cold, in the summer they are scorched by the sunshine. Will you not come and cover them?""I cannot leave the pond," cried the water-lily. "I cannot leave the moss," said the violet. "I cannot leave the green fields," said the daisy.

The little heather was trembling with eagerness. "If the great, beautiful mountain would only let me come," she thought and at last she whispered very softly and shyly, "Dear mountain, will you let me come? I have not any blossoms like the others, but I will try to keep the wind and the sun away from you."

"Let you!" cried the mountain. "I shall be very happy if you will only come."

The heather soon covered the rocky mountainside with her bright green, and the mountain called proudly to the other plants: "See how beautiful my little heather is." The others replied, "Yes, she is bright and green, but she has no blossoms."

But the next day, the little heather was bright with many blossoms, and blossoms she has had from that day to this.

—Legend

33

The Brook

I come from haunts of coot and hem,
I make a sudden sally
And sparkle out among the fern
To bicker down a valley.

By thirty hills I hurry down,
Or slip between the ridges,
By twenty thorps, a little town,
And half a hundred bridges.

I chatter over stony ways,
In little sharps and trebles,
I bubble into eddying bays,
I babble on the pebbles.

With many a curve my banks I fret,
By many a field and fallow,
And many a fairy foreland set
With willow-weed and mallow.

I chatter, chatter, as I flow
To join the brimming river,
For men may come and men may go,
But I go on for ever.

I wind about, and in and out
With here a blossom sailing,
And here and there a lusty trout
And here and there a grayling.

And here and there a foamy flake
Upon me, as I travel
With many a silvery waterbreak
Above the golden gravel,
And draw them all along, and flow
To join the brimming river,
For men may come and men may go,
But I go on for ever.

I slip, I slide, I gloom, I glance
Among the skimming swallows;
I make the netted sunbeams dance
Against my sandy shallows.

I murmur under moon and stars
In brambly wildernesses;
I linger by my shingly bars;
I loiter round my cresses;

And out again I curve and flow
To join the brimming river,
For men may come and men may go,
But I go on for ever.

—*Alfred Lord Tennyson*

Come Unto These Yellow Sands

Come unto these yellow sands,
And then take hands;
Curtsied when you have, and kissed.
The wild waves whist,
Foot it neatly here and there;
And sweet sprites the burden bear.
Hark, hark!
Bow, wow,
The watch dogs bark;
Bow wow,
Hark, hark! I hear
The strain of strutting chanticleer
Cry Cock-a-diddle-dow.

—*William Shakespeare*

Hie Away!

Hie away! hie away!
Over bank and over brae,
Where the copsewood is the greenest,
Where the fountains glisten sheenest,
Where the lady fern grows strongest,
Where the morning dew lies longest,
Where the black cock sweetest sips it,
Where the fairy latest trips it;
Hie to haunts right seldom seen,
Lovely, lonesome, cool and green;
Over bank and over brae
Hie away! hie away!

—*Sir Walter Scott*

Full Fathom Five

Full fathom five thy father lies,
Of his bones are corals made;
Those are pearls which were his eyes,
Nothing of him that doth fade
But doth suffer a sea change
Into something rich and strange.
Sea nymphs hourly ring his knell-Ding dong.
Hark now I hear them, ding dong bell.

—*William Shakespeare*

The Seal Woman

IN THE SEAS around the islands of Scotland, dwell the Selkie folk, who inhabit the bodies of grey seals; but when they come ashore, they cast aside their skins and appear in human form.

Once long ago on the island of Orkney, there lived a rich young farmer, who was known as the Goodman of Wastness. Everything he touched prospered and many of the maidens thereabouts would gladly have become his wife, but he would have none of them. One evening he went down to the shore at the ebb-tide. Some way out there was a half-submerged rock on which a company of folk were sunning themselves and splashing and playing in the shallow water. The Goodman was astonished to see people about in a spot that was usually deserted, and creeping nearer, he gazed at them curiously. What was his surprise to discover that they were Selkie folk who had come to enjoy the evening sunshine. Wishing to see them near at hand, he crept quietly up to the rock and leapt suddenly among them. With cries of terror, the Selkies seized their skins and plunged into the water, but in the confusion, the Goodman managed to lay hold of a skin which he tucked firmly under his arm. As he looked out to sea, he saw the heads of grey seals gazing at him from the waves and among them, he thought he saw a human head; but after a moment it disappeared and he turned back towards the shore, still carrying the skin. After a time he heard the sound of sobbing and turning round he beheld the loveliest maiden he had ever seen. She gazed at him beseechingly with the tears streaming down her face.

"Give me back my skin," she sobbed. "I cannot live in the water among my own folk without it. Oh give it back, I pray you!"

The Goodman's heart was filled with pity for the beautiful maiden, but at the same time, he longed to have her for his wife. Grasping the skin more firmly, he begged her to come and live with him. He pleaded so tenderly, yet fervently, that at last she consented and went home with him to his farm, where she became his wife and bore him seven fine children. They all lived together in great happiness.

So many years passed; then, one day, the Goodman and his three eldest sons went out fishing and the other children went to the shore to look for whelks. The seal woman sat down to her spinning wheel; presently she got up to fetch more wool from the store room. As she moved the heap, she saw a small chest in the corner which she did not remember to have seen before. She opened the lid and saw something soft and grey; she pulled it out; it was her seal skin. At the sight of it such a deep longing arose in her heart for her own people, that she felt she must go to them. She was sorrowful at the thought of leaving her children, but could not resist the call of the Selkie folk. She hastened down to the shore, where she quickly put on her skin and plunged into the sea.

As the Goodman and his three sons were pulling for the shore, they saw the heads of some grey seals rise up from the water. One pulled aside her skin from her face and the Goodman recognised his wife.

"Farewell, farewell, you have been a good husband to me, but now I must return to my own people." So saying she sank beneath the waves.

"Come back, come back," cried the Goodman in a voice filled with grief, but he saw her no more.

Often in the evening, he would go down to the shore and call to his wife, but although he sometimes saw the heads of grey seals in the distance, she never returned.

—*Scottish Folk Tale*

Cap O' Rushes

 NCE UPON A TIME there was a King who had three daughters and he wanted to find out how fond they were of him. So he called them all together and said to the eldest: "How much do you love me?" "I love you as I love my life," she replied. Then he asked the second. "How much do you love me? "

"I love you better than all the world," she answered.

Then he asked the youngest. "How much do you love me?"

"I love you as fresh meat loves salt," she said.

Then the King was very angry. "You do not love me at all!" he cried. "And you shall not stay in my palace." So he drove her forth and left her to wander.

After a time, she came to a fen where many rushes grew; these she gathered and made herself a cloak with a hood to cover her face. Her fine clothes were thus hidden and on she went till she came to a palace, where she enquired if they wanted a maid. At first they answered "No," but when they heard that she had nowhere to go and was not asking any wages and would do any kind of work, they said she might stay and wash the pots and scrape the saucepans.

So she stayed and did all the dirty work and since she would not tell her name, they called her Cap o' Rushes.

One day there was to be a grand dance at the palace and all the servants were allowed to go and look on and see the grand folk; but Cap o' Rushes said she was too tired and would go to bed. But when they had all gone, she took off her cap o' rushes, quickly dressed herself and went to the dance. When the King's son saw her, he fell in love with her at once, and would dance with no one else.

Before the dance was ended, Cap o' Rushes slipped away and returned to her attic room and when the other maids came back, she pretended to be asleep with her cap o' rushes on.

Next morning they told her of the beautiful princess who had appeared at the ball, and of how the prince could not take his eyes off her.

"I would like to have seen her," said Cap o' Rushes.

"Well," they answered, "there is to be another dance tonight and perhaps she will come."

But when evening came, Cap o' Rushes said she was too tired to go and the others went without her. Then she took off her cap o' rushes, dressed herself and went to the dance, where the Prince again danced with her all the time and would look at no one else. Before the ball was over, she slipped away and when the other maids came, she was lying in bed in her cap o' rushes, pretending to be asleep. Next morning they again told her of the beautiful princess and how the Prince danced with no one else.

"I should have liked to have seen her," said Cap o' Rushes.

"Well," they said, "there is another dance this evening and she is sure to be there." But when evening came Cap o' Rushes was too tired to go and said she would go to bed. When the others had gone, however, she jumped up, dressed herself and went to the ball. The Prince was delighted to see her coming and danced only with her. He begged her to tell him her name and where she came from, but she wouldn't. Then he gave her a ring and said he would die if he did not see her again, but once more she gave him the slip and ran off home, and when the other maids came back, she was in bed pretending to be asleep.

Next day they told her again of the beautiful princess. "That was the last dance," they said. "Now you will not see her."

"I wish I had seen her," said Cap o' Rushes.

The Prince tried in every way he could think of to find out who the beautiful Princess was and where she had gone, but no one knew her or had ever heard of her before. At last he became ill for love of her and had to keep his bed.

"You must make gruel for the Prince," they said to the cook. "He is dying for love of the unknown Princess." As she was making it, Cap o' Rushes came into the kitchen.

"What are you doing? "she asked.

"I'm making gruel for the Prince, he's dying of love for the Princess."

"Let me make it," said Cap o' Rushes.

At first the cook refused, but Cap O' Rushes begged so hard that at last she gave in and Cap o' Rushes made the gruel. When it was ready, she dropped the ring into it before the cook took it upstairs.

The Prince drank it and there was the ring at the bottom. He sent at once for the cook and asked her who had made the gruel.

"I did," she replied, for she was frightened.

"No, you didn't," said the Prince, looking at her. "Speak the truth and no harm shall befall you."

So at last the cook confessed that it was Cap o' Rushes, and the Prince commanded that she should be brought. When she appeared he asked, "Did you make my gruel?" "I did," she replied. "Where did you get the ring?" said the Prince. "I will show you," said Cap o' Rushes, and she took off her cap and cloak and stood there in her beautiful clothes.

The Prince soon recovered and the wedding was arranged. It was to be a very grand one and everyone was invited from far and near, including the King, Cap o' Rushes' father; but before the feast, Cap o' Rushes gave orders to the cook that she was to put no salt into any of the dishes.

Well, the wedding day came and they were married and afterwards all the company sat down to dinner. When they began to eat the meat it was so tasteless that they could not swallow it. After Cap o' Rushes' father had tried one dish after another, he began to weep.

"What is the matter?" asked the Prince.

"Ah," said the King, "once I had a daughter and I asked her how much she loved me. She replied, "I love you as fresh meat loves salt." And I thought she didn't love me at all and turned her from my door. But now I see that she loved me the best and I don't know where she is. She may be dead for aught I know."

"No, father, she is not dead; here she is," cried Cap o' Rushes, and she put her arms around him.

And so they all lived happily ever afterwards.

—*English Folk Tale*

40

The Night

The Sun descending in the west,
The evening star does shine;
The birds are silent in their nest,
And I must seek for mine.
The moon, like a flower
In heaven's high bower
With silent delight
Sits and smiles at the night.

Farewell green fields and happy groves,
Where flocks have took delight.
Where lambs have nibbled, silent moves
The feet of angels bright;
Unseen they pour blessing,
And joy without ceasing,
On each bud and blossom
And each sleeping bosom.
They look in every thoughtless nest,
Where birds are covered warm;
They visit caves of every beast,
To keep them all from harm.
If they see any weeping
That should have been sleeping
They pour sleep on their head
And sit down by their bed.

When wolves and tigers howl for prey,
They pitying stand and weep;
Seeking to drive their thirst away,
And keep them from the sheep.
But if they rush dreadful
The angels, most heedful
Receive each mild spirit
New worlds to inherit.

And there the lion's ruddy eyes
Shall flow with tears of gold
And pitying the tender cries,
And walking round the fold,
Saying "Wrath, by his meekness
And by his health, sickness
Is driven away
From our immortal day.

"And now beside thee, bleating lamb,
I can lie down and sleep;
Or think on him who bore thy name,
Graze after thee and weep.
For, washed in life's river,
My bright mane for ever
Shall shine like the gold
As I guard o'er the fold."

—*William Blake*

Matthew, Mark, Luke and John

Matthew, Mark, Luke and John
Bless the bed that I lie on.
Four corners to my bed,
Four angels round it spread,
One to watch and one to pray
And two to bear my soul away.

—*Old Rhyme*

The Twelve Apostles

THREE HUNDRED YEARS before the birth of the Lord Christ, there lived a mother who had twelve sons; but she was so poor that she did not know how to find food for them any longer. Every day she prayed to God to grant her that all her sons should be on earth together with the Saviour who was to come.

At last she could no longer feed them, and one by one she had to send them out into the world to gain a living. The oldest son was called Peter; he went away and had already gone a long distance, a whole day's journey, when he came to a thick wood, where he lost himself.

He searched for a way out, but could not find one, and went more and more astray. At the same time he felt such pangs of hunger that he could hardly keep upright. At last he felt so weak that he had to lie down and thought his death was near. Suddenly a child stood beside him, who was as radiant and beautiful as an angel. The child clapped his hands to make him look up, and said: "Why are you so sad?"

"O," answered Peter, "I wander through the world seeking food so that I may live to see the Lord when he comes down to earth; this is my greatest wish." The child said: "Come with me and your wish shall be fulfilled."

He took Peter's hand and led him between the rocks to a large cave. When they entered all within sparkled and glistened with gold, silver and crystal. In the middle twelve cradles were standing side by side. Then the angel said: "Lie down in the first cradle and sleep a little."

Peter did so, and the angel rocked him till he slept.

And while he slept the second brother came. He too was led there by his guardian angel, and he too was rocked to sleep like the first brother; and in the same way all the brothers came, one after the other, until all twelve lay asleep in the golden cradles.

There they slept for three hundred years until the night when the Saviour was born. Then they awoke and were with Him on the earth, and were called the twelve Apostles.

—Brothers Grimm

43

The Christmas Rose

ON CHRISTMAS EVE, the Christ child lay asleep on the straw of the manger. The mother Mary stepped outside the door of the stable and looked up to the dark skies. She wanted to bring her little son a greeting from the stars, so that in His joy He would forget His longing for His heavenly home. She was looking for star-flowers; they would best remind the child. Wrapped in her blue cloak, the mother Mary walked through the woods. But the ground was hard and frozen and nowhere could she discover a flower. She grew very sad. In her sorrow she did not notice how the angels of the clouds spread their heavy wings before the starry eyes of heaven; and how one snowflake after another flew down to the earth, till her blue cloak was covered with white.

Suddenly she heard a faint whisper near her ear. A snowflake had fallen into her hair and whispered softly: "We are sad that you do not notice us, and that you look in vain for starflowers on the frozen ground. We come from your child's starry home. Please look at us carefully. Could you find lovelier and more delicate stars? We would like to greet your child from His heavenly home, but you do not love us."

"Yes, I do love you, you little messengers of the stars," the mother Mary said happily. She knelt down and took up in her hand a small piece of the frozen earth, which she raised to the sky. Then many, many snowstars settled on it.

Carefully the mother Mary carried the starry greeting back to the stable. Quietly she closed the stable door behind her and went towards the manger, hiding her gift in her cloak. The child Jesus had just woken up and smiled at His mother. She opened her cloak a little, and let her child look in where her hand still concealed the snow-covered earth. But as the child looked with the wonderful radiance of His eyes, a strange thing happened. The snow began to shape itself. In the mother's warm hand the icy earth had thawed and tender roots stretched into it. And where the golden rays from the child's eyes shone into the blue shadow of the cloak, green stalks and leaves began to grow, and on the top a snow-white flower. But the most wonderful thing was the golden calyx that formed itself from the child's golden glance. The christmas-rose had appeared.

Since that time God has let it grow every year at Christmas. You find it, as it unfolds, in snow and ice. Then look at the bud, and your hearts will be filled with reverence for you will see, surrounded by a snow-white cup, the golden rays which had once come from the eyes of the child Jesus, when His mother brought Him greeting from His heavenly home.

—*Caroline Von Heydebrand*

The Sun Is in My Heart

The sun is in my heart,
He warms me with his power,
And wakens life and love
In bird and beast and flower.

The stars above my head
Are shining in my mind,
As spirits of the world
That in my thoughts I find.

The earth whereon I tread
Lets not my feet go through,
But strongly doth uphold
The weight of deeds I do.

Then must I thankful be
That man on earth I dwell,
To know and love the world
And work all creatures well.

—A. C. Harwood

Mary on the Flight into Egypt

MARY, ON HER FLIGHT into Egypt, had lost her way in a dark wood, and only late at night she found her way out and came to a little village.

There she knocked at the door of a big farm-house. "Who is there?" asked the farmer's wife, looking out of the window. "Please let me and my child come in just for this one night. We have come from far, and are very tired and cold."

"My house is not a tavern. See where else you can get shelter," was the answer, and sadly Mary and the child went on.

Suddenly she noticed a miserable little hut, from which there came a glimmer of light. Here also she knocked. "Come in," said a voice from within and when Mary entered, a poor woman asked in a friendly way what she would like. Mary begged for a night's shelter. "Gladly," said the woman, and after she had given them milk and bread, she prepared for them a comfortable bed.

When Mary continued her way the next morning, she thanked the woman, and said: "Whatever you do first today shall be rewarded unto you a thousandfold."

The poor woman quickly went to her spinning wheel, and began to spin busily all day, and when she looked at her work in the evening she noticed with joy and wonder that she had spun a thousand yards.

Some time after, when Mary returned from Egypt on the same way, she again met the hard-hearted woman, who had once refused to give her shelter for the night; when she saw Mary she went out to her, and asked her in a very kind manner if she would be her guest. For she had heard of the reward which the poor woman had received. Mary followed her into the house, and was served with the most delicious food; and afterwards she and her child were given a good, soft bed.

When Mary continued her journey the next morning, she thanked her and said: "Whatever you do first today shall be rewarded unto you a thousandfold." When the rich woman heard this, she was beside herself with joy and thought and thought what she should do. But the more she thought, the less she could think of. At last she hit her head in anger. This was the first thing she did that day, and as punishment for her hard-heartedness she continued a thousand times, until she could neither see nor hear.

—Legend

When Icicles Hang by the Wall

When icicles hang by the wall,
And Dick the Shepherd blows his nail,
And Tom bears logs into the hall,
And milk comes frozen home in pail:
When blood is nipped and ways be foul,
Then nightly sings the staring owl,
To-whit, to-whoo
A merry note,
While greasy Joan doth keel the pot.

When all aloud the wind doth blow,
And coughing drowns the parson's saw;
And birds sit brooding in the snow,
And Marian's nose is red and raw;
When roasted crabs hiss in the bowl,
Then nightly sings the staring owl,
To-whit, to-whoo
A merry note,
While greasy Joan doth keel the pot.

—*William Shakespeare*

47

The Three Sillies

THERE ONCE was a maiden who was so foolish that nobody wanted to marry her. One day, however, there arrived a young man to woo her, and her mother, full of joy, sent her downstairs to the cellar to draw a jug of beer. The girl did not come back, and after waiting for some time, the mother went to see what had happened to her, and found her sitting on the stairs, her head in her hands, while the beer ran out of the cask all over the floor as she had forgotten to turn the tap off.

"What are you doing?" asked the mother.

"If I marry that young man and have a child, what shall I call it? All the names in the calendar are taken already. That is what is troubling me."

"I will help you to think about it," said the mother and sat down beside her daughter.

Meanwhile the father began to wonder why neither his wife nor daughter returned with the beer, so presently he too went down to see what had happened. He found them both sitting on the stairs with the beer running all over the floor.

"What are you doing? The beer is running out!"

"We are thinking what to call the children our daughter will have when she marrys: the young man upstairs. All the names in the calendar have been taken already."

"Dear, dear," said the father. "I will help you to think." So he sat down with them on the stairs.

The young man waited and waited, but when neither the father, mother nor daughter returned, he decided to go and look for them. He found them all three sitting in the cellar while the beer ran all over the floor.

"What in the world are you doing?" he asked in astonishment. "Why have you not turned off the tap?"

"Oh my dear young man," said the father, "we are trying to think what you can call your children when you are married to our daughter; all the names in the calendar are taken."

"Well, upon my word," exclaimed the young man. "I could never have believed that anyone could be so silly! Goodbye, I am going away to look for three people sillier than you are, and if I find them I will come back and marry your daughter."

So off he went and when he had walked for some time, he came to an orchard where a man was knocking down walnuts and trying to throw them into a cart with a fork.

"What are you doing there?" he asked.

"I want to load the cart with walnuts but I can't do it."

"Why don't you get a basket, put the walnuts into it and then empty it into the cart?"

" Oh, what a good idea! Thank you, I'll do that!" he cried.

"Well," said the young man, as he walked away, "I have already found someone more foolish than those three."

On he went until he came to a wood where there was a man who wanted to give his pig some acorns and was trying to make it climb the oak tree.

"What are you doing?" asked the young man.

"I am trying to make my pig climb up to get some acorns but he won't," said the man.

"Why don't you shake the tree so that the acorns fall down, then the pig could pick them up from the ground?"

"Why, of course! What a good idea. I never thought of it."

"There is the second fool," said the young man to himself and went on his way. After a time he came to a man who had never worn any trousers and was trying to put on a pair. He had tied them to a tree and was jumping as high as he could into the air so that he should hit the two legs as he came down.

"Why don't you hold them like this in your hands and step into them, one leg at a time?" said the young man.

"Well, well, to be sure, that's the way. You are sharper than I, for I never thought of it."

Having found three people more foolish than his bride and her father and mother, he returned to the house to marry the daughter.

And in course of time they had a great many children.

—*English Folk Tale*

49

The Wise Men of Gotham

1.
Of Drowning Eels

When Lent was past, the men of Gotham consulted together as to what they should do with the salt fish that was left over. After much thought, they decided that all the fish, red herrings, white herrings, and sprats should be cast into the pond in the middle of the town so that they might breed for the next year.

"Let us all cast in our salt fish," said they, "then we shall have plenty and to spare next year."

At the beginning of the next year, the men went to the pond with nets to catch their fish, but they found nothing but one great eel.

"Oh," they said, "this wicked old eel has eaten all our fish. Plague take him!" "What shall we do to him?" asked one.

"Kill him."

"Chop him in pieces."

"Nay," said another, "let us drown him."

"Yes," cried all, "we will drown him."

So they went to another pond and threw in the eel.

"Lie there," they said, "for we will not help you." And they left the eel to drown.

2.
Of Selling Cheeses

There was once a man of Gotham who went off to the market at Nottingham to sell cheeses. As he was going down the hill towards Nottingham bridge, one of the cheeses fell out of his wallet and rolled down the hill.

"Oho," said the man, "you can go by yourself, can you? I will send the others after you."

And he put down his wallet and rolled one cheese after another down the hill.

"You shall all meet me in the market place," he shouted after them.

He went on his way and came to the market place and sat down to wait for his cheeses, but they never came.

Presently the market was over and people began to pack up their goods. Then the fellow went round to his friends and neighbours to inquire if they had seen his cheeses coming to market.

"Who was bringing them?" asked one.

"Why, they were bringing themselves," said the man, "they know the way. But I fear that they ran so fast that they have gone past the market and are now nearly at York."

So he hired a horse to ride to York, but he did not find his cheeses and to this day no one can tell him where they are.

3.
The Lost Fisher

Once twelve men of Gotham went a-fishing; some waded in the water and some stayed on dry land. When they were going home, one said to another, "We have ventured much in wading in the water; I pray none of us be drowned." "Yes, indeed," said his friend, "let us count ourselves." So they counted, but as each forgot to count himself, they could only count eleven. "Alas," they cried, "One of us must be drowned." They all went back to the brook and sought up and down, weeping, but could find nobody.

Presently a man came by and asked what was the matter. They told him the sad story with much lamentation, whereupon he said, "What will you give me if I find the twelfth man?" "Why," they replied, "we will give you all the money we have." "Here then," he said, giving one a blow on the shoulder, "is the first." So he did to each and at the last one he cried, "And here is the twelfth!" "Thank you, thank you," they exclaimed in joy, "and may God bless you. You have found our missing comrade."

Jack the Cunning Thief

THERE WAS ONCE a poor farmer who had three sons, who all set out to seek their fortunes. The two eldest were sober hardworking young men but the youngest had never done much. He loved to play tricks on people. The three parted when they came to cross roads and Jack took the loneliest. The day was rainy and he was wet and weary when night fell and he came to a house at which he knocked. It was a lonesome place, a little off the road and the door was opened by an old woman. "What do you want?" she asked.

"My supper and a bed," said Jack.

"You can't have it," said she.

"And who will stop me?" said he.

"The owners of the house," said she. "Six honest men and when they find you here they'll skin you alive."

"Skin me or not," said Jack, "I'm coming in, so get me something out of the cupboard."

So she gave him some supper and he went to bed. In the morning there were six ugly-looking men round his bed.

"Who are you?" said the chief, "and what do you want?"

"My name is Master Thief," said Jack, "and I want to find some workmen. If you are any good, I will give you some lessons maybe."

The six men were rather surprised and at last the head man said, "Well, get up and after breakfast we'll see who is to be master."

So Jack got up and just as they finished breakfast, they saw a farmer going by driving a fine large goat to market.

"Which of you," said Jack, "will steal that goat from the owner before he gets out of the wood and that without violence?"

But no one would undertake it.

"I am your master," said Jack, "and I'll do it."

He slipped out of the house, ran through the wood to where there was a bend in the road, and laid his right shoe in the middle of it. Then he ran on to the next bend where he laid down his left shoe and hid himself. Along came the farmer and when he saw the first shoe he said, "Well, here's a good shoe but it's no use by itself," and on he went. Presently he came to the second shoe. "Now why didn't I pick up the first?" he said. "I'll go back for it." So he tied up his goat to the hedge and set off back along the road. Meanwhile Jack had put on the first shoe and as soon as the man was out of sight he put on the second, untied the goat and led it back to the house.

The poor farmer looked and looked but couldn't find the first shoe and when at last he came back he couldn't find the second nor his goat.

"Whatever shall I do?" he said. "I promised my wife Joan to buy her a shawl. I must go back and drive another beast to market without her knowing. She mustn't find out what a fool I've made of myself."

The thieves were full of admiration for Jack and wanted him to tell them how he had deceived the farmer, but he wouldn't. Presently they saw the same man driving a fine fat sheep to market.

"Who will steal the sheep before it's out of the wood," said Jack, "and no violence?"

"Not I," said one. "Not I," said another.

"I will," said Jack. "Give me some rope."

The farmer was thinking of his loss when he saw a man hanging from the branch of a tree.

"Lord save us!" he said, "that man wasn't there an hour ago." After he had gone about a quarter of a mile, he saw another man hanging.

"Bless me!" he said, "am I in my right senses?"

Soon there was another turn in the road and when he had got round it, there was a third man hanging.

"I must be mad," said the farmer, "there couldn't be three men hanging. I'll go back and see if the other two are there still."

But as soon as he was round the bend, down came the hanged man, untied the sheep and made off with it. After a time back came the poor farmer having found no men dead or alive and here was his sheep gone too.

"Oh mercy me!" he cried. "What will I do now? Whatever will Joan say to me? I've lost both goat and sheep and my time into the bargain. I must sell something to get the price of the shawl. I'll take the fat bullock that's in the field, she won't see me driving it off."

Meanwhile Jack had arrived at the robbers' house with the sheep. They were astonished at his cleverness.

"Do another trick like that," said the chief, "and you shall be our captain." Soon the farmer went past again driving a fat bullock.

"Who can get the bullock with no violence?" asked Jack. But no one would undertake it. "I will," said Jack and off he went into the forest.

Just when the farmer was at the place where he had found the first shoe, he heard the bleating of a goat in the wood. He listened for a minute and then heard the baaing of a sheep.

53

"Maybe they're my own," he said. "I'll go and look," and he tied up the bullock to the hedge and went after the cries in the wood. But they always seemed a little in front of him and he followed on and on until they stopped altogether. He searched about but could find nothing so he came back for his bullock only to find it gone.

This time when the thieves saw Jack returning with the bullock, they shouted, "Jack must be our chief," and the rest of the day was spent in feasting; but at nightfall they showed Jack the cave where they kept their treasure.

One morning about a week later, while they were at breakfast they said to Jack, "Will you mind the house while we go to the fair in the town?" "Yes, I will," said Jack. So off they went.

As soon as they were gone Jack said to the old woman: "Do those fellows ever give you anything?"

"Not a halfpenny," she replied.

"Well, come with me," said Jack, "and I'll make you a rich woman."

He took her to the treasure cave and while she was gazing at the silver and gold, he quickly filled his pockets with as much as they would hold, put some more in a little bag, and slipped out, locking the door on the old woman, but leaving the key in the lock. Then he put on a rich suit of clothes, took the goat, the sheep and the bullock and drove them to the farmer's house. The farmer and his wife were at the door and when they saw the animals, they clapped their hands for joy.

"Do you know who owns these beasts?" asked Jack.

"Indeed I do, they're ours!"

"I found them straying in the wood. Is that bag of money round the goat's neck yours?"

"No, that it isn't."

"Well, you may as well keep it, I don't want it."

"Heaven bless you, good gentleman!"

Jack went on until at last he came to his father's house in the dusk of the evening.

He went in and said, "God save all in the house."

"And God save you, good sir."

"What, don't you know your own son?"

Well then you can imagine how they greeted him and kissed and hugged each other all round, and when they saw his riches they were still happier and lived from that day in great comfort.

—*Irish Folk Tale*

How a Little Flower Got Its Name

GOD WAS CREATING the world. He called a name and instantly whatever He had called sprang forth; stone or star, animal or tree. Everything softly repeated its name a few times so that it should remember it. Only the cuckoo is so stupid that he must still say it aloud so as not to forget it. Most of them learned it at once and they need to know it, for each spring God calls them again, one after the other. "Snowdrop!" and immediately it pushes up from the ground. "Violet!" and a sweet scent arises from the hedgerows. "Primrose!" and the mossy banks turn yellow. And so it goes on. It would be dreadful if a flower forgot its name and did not come when called.

And yet, one flower did forget her name. What it really was no one knows. She had just opened her blue petals and the name God had given her was sounding in her heart, when suddenly along came a blue butterfly and settled upon her. It was strange enough that the butterfly should be just as blue as she was, but the most wonderful thing was the lower part of his wings, for they were covered with tiny eyes. The flower could not stop wondering and when at last the butterfly flew away, she had forgotten her name!

How frightened she was! And it was still more dreadful when she saw God in the meadow asking each thing for its name. They all remembered, not one had forgotten. The poor little flower would have liked to sink into the earth, she hung her head for shame. But God did not scold her; He knew at once what had happened and said: "You have forgotten your name, have you not? Never mind, but—" and here He looked at her intently, "forget me not."

God had gone far away, but still the little flower remembered His words," Forget me not," and this became her new name. And so she always looks up to God so that she may never forget Him.

—*Michael Bauer*

The Violet

N A WOOD, where the sun peeped through the branches of the trees, there grew a violet. It was a modest little violet and it grew under a tree with big leaves; through an opening it could look up to the blue sky which it saw for the first time as it had just opened that morning. Now the violet was very frightened when it saw the blue sky, but it did not know why. Just then a dog ran past, a bad dog, and the violet said to him, "Tell me, what is that up there, that blue thing that looks like me?" For the sky was blue like the violet. The wicked dog answered, "Oh, that is a huge violet and it has grown so big so that it can hit you."

The poor little violet was still more frightened for it believed what the dog had said. It drew its petals together and hid under a big leaf which a gust of wind had just blown down from the tree. It stayed there all day, hiding from the big sky violet.

Next morning the little violet crept out, it had not slept at all for it had been thinking all night about the big blue violet. But it was not tired, it was quite fresh—violets get tired when they sleep and not when they stay awake. The first thing it saw was the rising sun and the rosy dawn and as it looked, it was no longer afraid but happy and joyful.

By and by as the dawn faded, the pale blue sky appeared. It grew bluer and bluer and the violet began to think again of what the dog had said about the big violet that wanted to hit it. Suddenly a lamb walked past and the violet thought it would ask again what that thing above it was. "What is that up there?" it said, and the lamb replied "That is a big blue violet like you." Now the violet was frightened again and thought the lamb would say the same thing as the bad dog. But the lamb was good and had such kind eyes that the violet ventured to ask again "Oh, dear lamb, will that great big violet up there hit me?"

"Oh no," answered the lamb, "it will not hit you, its love is as much greater than yours as it is bluer than your tiny self."

Then the violet understood at once that the big violet did not want to hurt it but would protect it from everything in the world that might harm it. And it was very happy. All the blue of the big sky violet seemed to it like God's love streaming down from all sides and the little violet always looked up as if it wanted to pray to the God of the violets.

—After Rudolf Steiner

Pippa's Song

The year's at the spring;
The day's at the morn;
Morning's at seven;
The hillside's dew-pearled,
The lark's on the wing,
The snail's on the thorn;
God's in his heaven-—
All's right with the world!

—*Robert Browning*

The Shepherd's Sweet Lot

How sweet is the shepherd's sweet lot!
From the morn to the evening he strays,
He shall follow his sheep all the day,
And his tongue shall be filled with praise.

For he hears the lambs' innocent call,
And he hears the ewes' tender reply.
He is watchful while they are in peace,
For they know when their shepherd is nigh.

—*William Blake*

Lines Written in March

The cock is crowing,
The stream is flowing,
The small birds twitter,
The lake doth glitter,
The green field sleeps in the sun;
The oldest and youngest
Are at work with the strongest.
The cattle are grazing
Their heads never raising,
There are forty feeding like one!
Like an army defeated
The snow hath retreated,
And now doth fare ill
On the top of the bare hill;
The plough boy is whooping-anon-anon;
There's joy in the mountains;
There's life in the fountains;
Small clouds are sailing,
Blue sky prevailing,
The rain is over and gone!

—William Wordsworth

The Lamb

Little lamb, who made thee?
Dost thou know who made thee?
Gave thee life and bid thee feed
By the stream and o'er the mead;
Gave thee clothing of delight
Softest clothing, woolly, bright;
Gave thee such a tender voice,
Making all the vales rejoice?
Little lamb who made thee?
Dost thou know who made thee?

Little lamb, I'll tell thee,
Little lamb, I'll tell thee;
He is called by thy name,
For He calls Himself a lamb.
He is meek and he is mild;
He became a little child.
I a child, and thou a lamb
We are called by his name.
Little lamb, God bless thee!
Little lamb, God bless thee!

—*William Blake*

The Echoing Green

The sun doth arise
And make happy the skies;
The merry bells ring
To welcome the spring.
The skylark and thrush
And the birds of the bush
Sing louder around
To the bells' cheerful sound;
While our sports shall be seen
On the echoing green.

Old John with white hair
Does laugh away care,
Sitting under the oak,
Among the old folk
They laugh at our play
And soon they all say,
"Such, such were the joys
When we all—girls and boys—
In our youth-time were seen
On the echoing green."

Till the little ones weary
No more can be merry;
The sun does descend
And our sports have an end.
Round the laps of their mothers
Many sisters and brothers
Like birds in their nest,
Are ready for rest,
And sport no more seen,
On the darkening green.

—William Blake

Spring

Spring, the sweet Spring, is the year's pleasant king,
Then blooms each thing, then maids dance in a ring,
Cold doth not sting, the pretty birds do sing
Cuckoo, jug-jug, pu-we, to-witta-woo!

The palm and may make country houses gay,
Lambs frisk and play, the shepherds pipe all day,
And we hear ay, birds tune this merry lay,
Cuckoo, jug-jug, pu-we, to-witta-woo!

The fields breathe sweet, the daisies kiss our feet,
Young lovers meet, old wives a-sunning sit,
In every street these tunes our ears do greet,
Cuckoo, jug-jug, pu-we, to witta-woo!
Spring! the sweet Spring!

—Thomas Nash

A Grace

The seeds are awakened in the darkness of earth,
The green leaves are quickened through the power of the air
And all fruits are ripened in the might of the sun.

So wakens the soul in the shrine of the heart,
So quickens the spirit in the light of the world,
So ripens man's strength in the glory of God.

—Rudolf Steiner

Saint Kevin and the Blackbird

AINT KEVIN was walking through the fields one day in spring. He looked at the fresh, green meadows, and the many colored flower stars, which spoke to him of their heavenly home! He listened to the birds' songs, and watched the young lambs play. How wonderful the world was! In his heart was a deep longing to thank the One who had made it so beautiful.

He knelt on the grass, and lifted his hands skywards. For many hours his soul was deep in prayer.

When he returned to ordinary life, and became again aware of the world around him, he felt something strange in his hand. Carefully bending his arm so as not to disturb whatever it was, he saw a nest with one light blue egg with pink spots. A blackbird mother had chosen the hollow of his calm hand as a home for her young. He would not disappoint her. Lifting his arm to the same position he decided to wait till the little birds would be old enough to fly.

A few minutes later the motherbird returned, and settling down on his hand laid another egg. At last there were four eggs. Only for short moments did the blackbird mother leave them.

Night and day Saint Kevin remained still. The people who had noticed his absence found him and brought him food. His beard and his hair grew long and bushy.

After fourteen days and nights, one morning in May he heard a gentle knock, the cracking of shells and a faint chirping; he felt something soft and wet.

Eggshells dropped from the nest. The mother flew away, and returned with a worm. To and fro she flew bringing many a worm or fly to feed the four little ones whose beaks were always open.

Then for the first time they ventured out of their nest, four awkward helpless little things; until one sunny summer day they all flew away.

Saint Kevin slowly got up. The fields were now yellow with the ripening corn, different flowers bloomed on the meadows. He bade a last farewell to the place he knew and loved so well, and then quietly took his way home.

—Legend

The Robin's Song

God bless the field and bless the furrow,
Stream and branch and rabbit burrow.
Hill and stone and flower and tree,
From Bristol town to Wetherby—
Bless the sun, and bless the sleet,
Bless the lane and bless the street,
Bless the night and bless the day
From Somerset and all the way
To the meadows of Cathay;
Bless the minnow: bless the whale,
Bless the rainbow and the hail,
Bless the nest and bless the leaf,
Bless the righteous and the thief.
Bless the wing and bless the fin,
Bless the air I travel in,
Bless the mill and bless the mouse,
Bless the miller's bricken house,
Bless the earth and bless the sea,
God bless you and God bless me!

—*Old English Rhyme*

Stories of St. Francis

Saint Francis Bids the Swallows Be Silent

ONE DAY SAINT FRANCIS came to the village of Todi, and wanted to preach to the people there. Before he began his sermon, he asked for silence. The people were quite still but though they listened most attentively, they could hardly hear a word, because of the noise of many swallows nesting nearby.

Then Saint Francis called out to them: "My sisters, dear swallows, now it is my turn to speak. Listen to the word of God, and wait till my sermon is ended."

Instantly, the swallows were silent, and did not move till Saint Francis had finished speaking.

All the people there present praised God with great wonder and this story was told all over the country, and the hearts of those who heard it were filled with reverence for Saint Francis.

 ## Saint Francis Preaches to the Birds

ONCE SAINT FRANCIS was walking along the road to Bevagna with two of his followers, when, looking up, he saw a crowd of birds sitting on the branches of some trees in a field. Saint Francis was surprised at this sight and said to his companions: "Wait here till I come back. I want to go and preach to my sisters, the birds."

And while his companions sat down, he went into the field and began to preach and all the birds flew down to him, and listened to his words; and this is what he said: "My little sisters, much do you owe to God who created you, and always and in every place, you should praise and thank Him: for He has given you a thick warm vesture. He has given you freedom to go into every place and you must thank Him for the element of air which He has appointed for you.

You do not sow, neither do you reap, and God feeds you, and gives you the mountains and the valleys for your refuge, and the tall trees wherein to build your nests, and forasmuch that you can neither spin nor sew, God clothes you and your children. Your Creator loves you much, who has dealt so bountifully with you; therefore beware, little sisters, of the sin of ingratitude, and strive ever to serve God."

While Saint Francis was thus speaking the birds began to open their beaks, stretched their necks, spread their wings and then reverently bowed their heads and showed through twittering and chirping how pleased they were with the holy father.

Saint Francis was not less pleased: he marvelled at their great number, and their manifoldness, their attention and affection. Reverently he praised the Creator in them. When he had finished Saint Francis made the sign of the cross over them, and allowed them to fly away.

Then they rose in the air singing their sweetest songs, and flew according to the cross which Saint Francis had made over them, one group to the east, one to the west; one to the south, and one to the north.

Saint Francis and the Wolf of Gubbio

NOT VERY FAR FROM Assisi was a little town called Gubbio, where Saint Francis sometimes used to stay. Once when he went there, he found the people panic-stricken, for a huge and fierce wolf had taken up his abode in the neighborhood. It was so bold, that it came prowling round the walls ready to seize any person who might be walking there. Once or twice it had even come into the town itself, and carried off a little child. No man dared venture abroad unless he were armed; women and children remained at home.

Saint Francis felt sorry for the people and he decided to go and find the wolf, though the citizens begged him not to attempt it. He left the town, entrusting his life to God.

As he approached its lair, the wolf fiercely rushed towards him, with open mouth and angry eyes. At the sight a loud cry came up from the people who stood watching at a distance.

Unafraid, Saint Francis waited till creature came quite near, then he made the sign of the cross over him and said: "Come hither, brother wolf. I command thee in the name of Christ, to do no harm, neither to me, nor to any man."

Then a great awe fell on the watching people, for the fierce beast instantly shut its mouth, the anger died out of its eyes and like a lamb it came and lay down at Saint Francis' feet.

And Saint Francis went on: "Brother wolf, much damage hast thou wrought, and done much evil when thou hast killed the creatures of God without His permission. Much terror and sorrow hast thou caused in the little city, for which thou deservest to be slain. But I believe that thou hast done all this because thou wast hungry, and hadst nothing to eat; so now will I make peace between thee and the citizens of Gubbio. They will provide thee with food, on condition thou wilt promise to do no harm either to man or beast. Dost thou promise?"

In answer the wolf bowed his head, then lifted his big paw, and put it into Saint Francis' hand, in token that he promised.

Then Saint Francis bade him return with him to Gubbio and there renew the promise in the sight of all the people. And the wolf, having made signs that he agreed, trotted along quietly by his side, through the vineyards and along the road which led into the city.

As the news spread, all the people of the town, men and women, crowded to the market place to see Saint Francis and the wolf. When everybody was gathered together Saint Francis turned to the people and said: "Brother wolf has promised to make peace with you and do you no more harm; I will pledge my word for him; will you on your part promise to feed him and be kind to him?"

Everyone promised to do so. Then he turned to the wolf: "Brother wolf, will you now promise to make peace with these people and to attack neither man nor beast?"

And once more the wolf bowed his head and placed his great paw in Saint Francis' hand.

After that the wolf lived two more years in Gubbio, and used to walk about like a tame creature from door to door doing hurt to no one, and no one doing hurt to him. He was kindly fed by the people, and as he walked about the town, never a dog barked at him.

At last, after two years, brother wolf died of old age, whereat the citizens grieved much, for when they beheld him thus tamely going about, they remembered better the virtues and holiness of Saint Francis.

Canticle to the Sun

Praised be God for brother Sun,
Who shines with splendid glow,
He brings the golden day to us,
Thy glory does he show!

Praised be God for sister Moon
And every twinkling star;
They shine in heaven most bright and clear,
All glorious they are.
Praised be God for brother Wind
That storms across the skies,
And then grows still, and silent moves,
And sweetly sings and sighs.

Praised be God for Water pure,
Her usefulness we tell,
So humble, precious, clean and good,
She works for us so well.

Praised be God for brother Fire
Friendly and wild and tame,
Tender and warm, mighty and strong,
A flashing, flaring flame.
Praised be God for mother Earth,
Who keeps us safe and well,
Whose mother heart all warm with love,
Dark in her depths doth dwell.

—Transcribed By Lawrence Edwards

The Larks at the Death of Saint Francis

LARKS LOVE THE LIGHT; they do not like the darkness; and yet late in the evening they flew in great numbers on to the roof of the convent where Saint Francis died. In spite of the late hour they rose high up into the sky singing their songs of praise.

Gratefully they sang a last farewell song for the old man as he had always invited them to praise God. Of all the birds he loved the larks most tenderly. They seemed to give in so many things the best example to his Brothers. Often he had asked his Brothers to watch the larks, who when they found only one grain of corn rose singing into the sky to thank their Creator. That is why he loved them so, and asked his Brothers to follow their example.

The Skylark

EARLY IN THE MORNING, when the sky turned from dark blue to white until it seemed on fire, and glowed in flaming red as a first morning greeting from the rising sun, a skylark soared singing up into the sky. Louder and louder grew his songs of welcome and joy, as the sun itself appeared and clothed everything with a radiant cloak of gold. Higher and higher he flew, a tiny speck in a golden sea till he almost disappeared.

A few moments later he sank deep down to the earth, and scuttled along the grass to his nest in the field.

A sleepy hedgehog, who saw him, said full of surprise to a mole who had only just woken up: "Look, here he comes like a messenger from heaven. How can he who lives with us in the furrows of the field rise to such heights?"

"Why does he, who can fly higher than any of us, build his nest so low?" twittered the birds up in the branches of the trees.

Might we not learn this from the sun? From the heights of heaven he greets every grain and seed in the deepest corners of the earth; and do not all the flowers thank him and grow, and are not all creatures happy in his rays? How can we love the earth without loving the sun?

While the hedgehog wondered and the birds chattered the skylark rose once more to the highest heights, joyfully singing his song of thanks, and then returned to his nest in the fields.

—*Elisabeth Gmeyner*

Laughing Song

When the green woods laugh with the voice of joy,
And the dimpling stream runs laughing by;
When the air does laugh with our merry wit,
And the green hill laughs with the noise of it;
When the meadows laugh with lively green,
And the grasshopper laughs in the merry scene;
When Mary and Susan and Emily,
With their sweet round mouths sing "Ha, ha, he! "

When the painted birds laugh in the shade,
When our table with cherries and nuts is spread;
Come live and be merry, and join with me
To sing the sweet chorus of "Ha, ha, he!"

—*William Blake*

Over Hill, Over Dale

Over hill, over dale,
Through bush, through brier,
Over park, over pale,
Through flood, through fire,
I do wander everywhere
Swifter than the moone's sphere,
And I serve the fairy queen,
To dew her orbs upon the green;
The cowslips tall her pensioners be;
In their gold coats spots you see;
Those be rubies, fairy favours,
In their freckles live their savours;
I must go seek some dewdrops here
And hang a pearl in every cowslip's ear.

—*William Shakespeare*

Where The Bee Sucks

Where the bee sucks, there suck I,
In a cowslip's bell I lie;
There I couch when owls do cry
On a bat's back I do fly
After summer merrily;
Merrily, merrily, shall I live now
Under the blossom that hangs on the bough.

—*William Shakespeare*

You Spotted Snakes

You spotted snakes with double tongue,
Thorny hedgehogs, be not seen;
Newts and blind worms do no wrong;
Come not near our fairy queen.
Philomel, with melody,
Sing in our sweet lullaby;
Lulla, lulla, lullaby; lulla, lulla, lullaby!
Never harm,
Nor spell nor charm,
Come our lovely lady nigh;
So, goodnight, with lullaby.

Weaving spiders, come not here,
Hence, you long-legged spinners, hence!
Beetles black, approach not near;
Worm nor snail, do no offence.
Philomel, with melody,
Sing in our sweet lullaby;
Lulla, lulla, lullaby; lulla, lulla, lullaby!
Never harm,
Nor spell nor charm,
Come our lovely lady nigh,
So, goodnight, with lullaby.

—*William Shakespeare*

Lusmore at Knockgrafton

HERE WAS ONCE a poor man who lived in a fertile glen at the foot of the gloomy Galtee mountains, and he had a great hump on his back; he looked just as if his body had been rolled up and placed upon his shoulders; and his head was pressed down with the weight of so much, that his chin, when he was sitting, used to rest upon his knees for support. The country people were rather shy of meeting him in any lonesome place, for though, poor creature, he was as harmless and inoffensive as a new-born infant, yet his deformity was so great that he scarcely appeared to be a human creature. He was said to have a great knowledge of herbs and charms; but certain it was that he had a mighty skillful hand in plaiting straw and rushes into hats and baskets, which was the way he made his livelihood. Lusmore, for that was the nickname put upon him by reason of his always wearing a sprig of the fairy cap or lusmore (the foxglove) in his little straw hat, would ever get a higher penny for his plaited work than anyone else. One evening, it happened that he was returning from the town, and as little Lusmore walked very slowly on account of the great hump on his back, it was quite dark when he came to the old moat of Knockgrafton, which stood on the right hand side of his road. Tired and weary was he, so he sat down under the moat to rest himself.

Presently there rose a wild strain of unearthly melody upon the ear of little Lusmore; he listened, and he thought he had never heard such ravishing music before. It was like the sound of many voices, each mingling and blending with the other so strangely that they seemed to be one, though all singing different strains, and the words of the song were these: Da Luan, Da Mort, Da Luan, Da Mort, Da Luan, Da Mort; when there would be a moment's pause and then the sound of melody went on again. Lusmore listened attentively; he now plainly perceived that the singing was within the moat; and though at first it had charmed him so much, he began to get tired of hearing the same round sung over and over without any change. So he waited till the pause came, when the Da Luan, Da Mort had been sung three times, and took up the tune, adding the words "Augus Da Cadine." Then he went on singing with the voices inside of the moat, Da Luan, Da Mort, finishing the melody when the pause came again, with Augus Da Cadine.

The fairies within Knockgrafton, for the song was a fairy melody, when they heard this addition to the tune, were so much delighted that they determined to bring the mortal among them, whose musical skill was so much greater than theirs, and little Lusmore was instantly whirled into their company.

71

Glorious to behold was the sight that met him as he came down through the moat, twirling round and round, with the lightness of a straw. The greatest honour was then paid him, he had servants tending upon him and everything to his heart's content, and in short he was made as much of as if he had been the first man in the land.

Presently Lusmore saw some of the fairies whispering together and he felt very much frightened in spite of their civility, until one stepping out from the rest came up to him and said:

> "Lusmore! Lusmore!
> Doubt not, nor deplore,
> For the hump which you bore
> On your back is no more;
> Look down on the floor,
> And view it, Lusmore!"

When these words were said, poor little Lusmore felt himself so light, and so happy, that he thought he could have bounded at one jump over the moon; and he saw his hump tumble down upon the ground from his shoulders. He then tried to lift up his head and looked round with the greatest wonder and delight upon everything which appeared more and more beautiful, till his head grew dizzy and his eyesight became dim. At last he fell into a sound sleep, and when he awoke he found that it was broad daylight, the sun shining brightly and the birds singing sweetly; and that he was lying just at the foot of the moat of Knockgrafton, with the cows and sheep grazing peacefully round about him. The first thing Lusmore did, after saying his prayers, was to put his hand behind to feel for his hump, but no sign of one was there on his back, and he looked at himself with great pride, for he had now become a well-shaped dapper little fellow, and more than that, found himself in a full suit of new clothes which he supposed the fairies had given him.

Towards home he went, stepping out lightly and springing up at every step. Not a creature who met Lusmore knew him without his hump and he had great work to persuade everyone that he was the same man.

Of course it was not long before the story of Lusmore's hump got about, and a great wonder was made of it. Through the country, for miles around it was the talk of everyone, high and low.

One morning as Lusmore was sitting contentedly at his cabin door, up came an old woman and asked him if he could direct her to one Lusmore, who, as she had heard, had had his hump taken off by the fairies.

"For," said she, "there is a son of a gossip of mine, who has got a hump on him that will be his death; and maybe if he could use the same charm as Lusmore, the hump may be taken off him. And now I have told you the reason of my coming so far: 'tis to find out about this charm, if I can."

Lusmore, who was ever a good-natured little fellow, told the woman all the particulars, how he had added to the song for the fairies at Knockgrafton, how his hump had been taken from his shoulders; and how he had got a new suit into the bargain. The woman thanked him very much, and then went away quite happy and easy in her own mind. When she came back to her gossip's house, she told her everything that Lusmore had said, and they put the little hump-backed man, who was a peevish and cunning creature from his birth, upon a cart, and took him all the way across the country. It was a long journey, but they did not care for that, so long as the hump was taken off him; and they brought him, just at nightfall and left him under the old moat of Knockgrafton.

Jack Madden, for that was the humpy man's name, had not been sitting there long, when he heard the tune going on within the moat much sweeter than before; for the fairies were singing it the way Lusmore had showed them, and the song was going on, Da Luan, Da Mort, Da Luan, Da Mort, Da Luan, Da Mort, Augus Da Cadine, without ever stopping.

Jack Madden, who was in a great hurry to get quit of his hump, never thought of waiting until the fairies had done, but having heard them sing it over seven times without stopping, out he bawls, never minding the time or the tune or how he could bring his words in properly, Augus Da Cadine, Augus Da Hena, thinking that if one day was good, two were better; and that if Lusmore had one new suit of clothes given him, he should have two.

No sooner had the words passed his lips than he was taken up and whisked roughly into the moat; and the fairies came crowding round him with great anger, screeching and screaming and roaring out, "Who spoiled our tune? Who spoiled our tune?" And one stepped up to him, above all the rest, and said:

"Jack Madden! Jack Madden!
Your words came so bad in
The tune we felt glad in,
That your life we may sadden,
Here's two humps for Jack Madden!"

73

And twenty of the strongest fairies brought Lusmore's hump and put it down upon poor Jack's back, over his own, where it became fixed as firmly as if it was nailed on with twelve penny nails, by the best carpenter that ever drove one. Out of their castle they kicked him; and, in the morning, when Jack, Madden's mother and her gossip came to look after the little man, they found him half dead, lying at the foot of the moat, with the other hump upon his back. Well, to be sure, how they did look at each other! But they were afraid to say anything, lest a hump might be put upon their shoulders. Home they brought the unlucky Jack Madden with them, as downcast in their hearts and their looks as ever two gossips were; and what with the weight of his other hump, and the long journey, he died after, leaving, they say, his heavy curse to anyone who would go to listen to fairy tunes again.

—*Irish Folk Tale*

When Cats Run Home

When cats run home and light is come,
And dew is cold upon the ground,
And the far-off stream is dumb,
And the whirring sail goes round,
And the whirring sail goes round;
Alone and warming his five wits
The white owl in the belfry sits.

When merry milkmaids click the latch,
And rarely smells the new-mown hay,
And the cock has sung beneath the thatch,
Twice or thrice his roundelay,
Twice or thrice his roundelay;
Alone and warming his five wits
The white owl in the belfry sits.

—*Alfred Lord Tennyson*

Meg Merrilies

Old Meg she was a Gipsy
And lived upon the Moors;
Her bed it was the brown heath turf,
And her house was out of doors,
Her apples were swart blackberries,
Her currants pods o' broom;
Her wine was dew of the wild white rose,
Her book a churchyard tomb.

Her Brothers were the craggy hills
Her Sisters larchen trees—
Alone with her great family
She lived as she did please.
No breakfast had she many a morn
No dinner many a noon,
And 'stead of supper she would stare
Full hard against the Moon.

But every morn of woodbine fresh
She made her garlanding,
And every night the dark glen yew
She wove and she would sing,
And with her fingers old and brown
She plaited mats o' rushes,
And gave them to the cottagers
She met among the bushes.

Old Meg was brave as Margaret Queen
And tall as Amazon;
An old red blanket cloak she wore;
A chip hat had she on.
God rest her aged bones somewhere—
She died full long agone!

—*John Keats*

Beauty and the Beast

ONCE UPON A TIME a rich Merchant, meeting with heavy losses, had to retire to a small cottage with his three daughters. The two elder grumbled at this, but the youngest, named Beauty, tried to comfort her father. Once when he was going on a journey, to try and mend his fortunes, the two elder girls told him to bring them some handsome presents, but Beauty begged him to bring her a rose. When the merchant was on his way back he saw some fine roses and thinking of Beauty, plucked the prettiest he could find. He had no sooner taken it, than he saw a hideous Beast, who asked him how he dared to touch his flowers and talked of putting him to death. The merchant pleaded that he had only plucked the rose for his daughter Beauty. "Well," said the Beast gruffly, "I will not take your life if you will bring one of your daughters here to die in your stead. She must come willingly, or I will not have her."

The merchant returned home in great sorrow. When he came near his house, his children came out to greet him, but seeing the sadness of his face, they asked the cause of his trouble. Giving Beauty the rose, he told her all. The two elder sisters laid all the blame on Beauty, who said that she alone must suffer as she was the cause of this misfortune and in spite of the entreaties of her father, she set out with him for the Beast's palace, to the secret joy of her two envious sisters.

When they arrived, the doors opened of themselves; sweet music was heard, and they walked into a room where supper was prepared. Just as they had finished their meal, the Beast entered and said in a mild tone, "Beauty, did you come here willingly?" "Willingly," she answered in a trembling voice. "So much the better for you," said the Beast. "Your father must return home tomorrow morning."

Beauty tried to cheer her father at parting, but he left her with a heavy heart. After he had gone, she began to explore the palace. She found a fine room, on the door of which was written in gold letters "Beauty's Room." All her meals were served to the sound of music and at supper time the Beast would appear and talk so pleasantly that she soon lost her fear of him. One day, he turned to her and said, "Am I so very ugly?" "Yes indeed you are," said Beauty, "but you are so kind that I do not mind your looks." "Will you marry me then?" asked he. Beauty, looking away, said, "Pray do not ask me." He then bade her good-night with a sad voice and retired.

The palace was full of beautiful rooms and Beauty had everything she could wish for, but except at supper time, she was always alone; the Beast then appeared and behaved so agreeably, that she liked him more and more. But when he asked, "Beauty, will you marry me?" she always replied, "No," on which he sadly took his leave.

Although Beauty had all she wanted, she was not happy, as she could not forget her father and sisters. At last, one evening, she begged so hard of the Beast to let her go home, that he agreed on her promising not to stay away longer than two months. He gave her a ring and told her to place it on her dressing table whenever she wished to go or to return and he also gave her presents to take home with her. The poor Beast looked sadder than ever when he said farewell to Beauty; she tried to cheer him, but nothing she said could comfort him. Beauty put the ring on her dressing table and fell asleep; next morning when she awoke, what was her joy at finding herself in her father's house with the gifts from the palace at her bedside.

Her father was overjoyed to see her again and her two sisters pretended to be glad, but were secretly jealous of her good fortune. Time passed very pleasantly, however, and whenever Beauty said she must return, her father begged her to stay a few days longer and she could not resist his entreaties. But one night, she dreamed that the poor Beast was lying dead in the palace garden; she awoke in a fright, looked for her ring and placed it on her dressing table. In the morning she was at the palace again, but the Beast was nowhere to be found. At last she ran to the place in the garden that she had dreamed about, and there, sure enough, was the poor Beast, lying on his back, senseless.

At this sight Beauty wept and reproached herself for having caused his death. She ran to a fountain and sprinkled his face with water. The Beast opened his eyes and as soon as he could speak, he said sorrowfully, "Now that I see you once more, I die contented." "No, no," she cried, "you shall not die! I will marry you!"

The moment she had uttered these words, a dazzling light shone everywhere, the palace windows glittered with lamps and music was heard around. To her great wonder a handsome young Prince stood before her, who said that her words had broken the spell of a magician, by which he had been doomed to take the form of a Beast until a beautiful girl should love him in spite of his ugliness. The grateful Prince now claimed Beauty as his wife. The merchant was soon informed of his daughter's good fortune, and the Prince was married to Beauty on the following day.

—*French Fairy Tale*

The Crystal Ball

HERE WAS ONCE A WITCH, who had three sons who loved one another dearly; but the old woman did not trust them, and thought they wanted to rob her of her power. She therefore changed the eldest into an eagle. He had to live high up among the rocks, and sometimes he could be seen soaring in great circles up in the sky. The second son she turned into a whale. He lived deep down in the sea and the men on the land only saw how from time to time he threw up a mighty spray of water. The third son was afraid that she might turn him too into a wild beast, perhaps into a bear or a wolf, so he stole away secretly.

He had heard however that in the Castle of the Golden Sun there was an enchanted princess waiting to be released; but everyone who attempted this had to risk his life. Already twenty-three youths had died a miserable death. Now there was only one more chance. And as his heart was without fear he resolved to seek the Castle of the Golden Sun.He had already been wandering for a long time and had not been able to find it, when he came into a forest in which he lost his way.

Suddenly he saw in the distance two giants. They waved to him and when he came up to them they said, "We are quarrelling over a hat and as we are both equally strong, neither can overcome the other. You little men are cleverer than we are and we will therefore leave you to decide who shall have it."

"How can you quarrel over an old hat?" said the youth.

"You do not know what sort of hat it is. It is a magic hat; he who puts it on can wish himself wherever he likes and in a moment he will be there."

"Give me the hat," said the youth. "I will go some distance away from you, and when I call you start running and the one who reaches me first shall have the hat."

He put the hat on and went away; but he thought of the princess, forgot all about the giants and went further and further. All at once he sighed from the bottom of his heart, "O if only I were at the Castle of the Golden Sun."

These words had hardly passed his lips when he found himself standing on a high mountain outside the castle gate.

He entered and went through all the rooms until in the last he found the princess. But how horrified he was when he looked at her. She had an ash grey face full of wrinkles, dull eyes, and red hair.

"Are you the princess whose beauty the whole world is praising?" he asked in amazement.

"O," she answered, "this is not my true form. The eyes of men can only see me in this ugly shape, but if you want to see me as I really am, look into this mirror which cannot be deceived; it will show me to you as I am in truth."

She handed him the mirror and in it he saw the most beautiful maiden in the world; tears of sorrow were flowing down her cheeks.

Then he said: "How can you be released? I fear no danger."

She answered: "He who gets the Crystal Ball and holds it out to the wizard will break with it his power and I shall return to my own form. Oh," she added, "many have already found their death. You are young, I feel sorry that you should enter upon all these dangers."

"Nothing can keep me back," he said, "but tell me what I must do."

"You shall know all," said the princess. "If you go down the hill on which the castle stands, a wild bull is waiting at the bottom near a spring. With him you must fight. And if you succeed in killing him, a fiery bird will rise from him, who bears in his body a glowing egg; this egg has as its yolk the Crystal Ball. But he will not drop the egg until he is forced to do so, and if it falls on the ground it will kindle and burn everything near it; the egg itself will melt, and with it the Crystal Ball; then all your trouble will have been in vain."

The youth went down to the spring where the bull was raging and roaring. After a long fight he thrust his sword through the bull's body, and it fell.

At once the fiery bird arose from it, and would have flown away; but the eagle who was the youth's brother, swooping down between the clouds, drove him toward the sea, so that in his haste he dropped the egg. It fell on to a fisherman's hut which stood on the shore. At once the hut began to smoke, and was about to go up in flames, when waves as high as houses suddenly arose from the sea; they streamed over the hut, and put out the fire. The other brother, the whale, had swum near and thrown up the water.

When the fire was quenched, the youth searched for the egg, and luckily he found it. It had not yet melted, but the shell had crumbled away through the sudden cold of the water, and he was able to take out the Crystal Ball unharmed.

When the youth went to the wizard holding the Crystal Ball in his hand, the wizard said: "My power is at an end; from now onward you are king of the Castle of the Golden Sun. You can also give back to your brothers their human form."

Then the youth hurried to the princess and when he entered her room, she stood there in all her radiant beauty. They were married and lived happily ever after.

—Brothers Grimm

The Cedar

THE CEDAR GREW UP between fir trees; it shared with them rain and sunshine, and grew high above their heads and looked far down into the valley.

Then the fir trees grumbled; "Is this how you thank us? We fed you when you were small and now you rise proudly above us."

"Complain to Him who made me grow."

Around the cedar stood many thornbushes. They were angry that he stood there glorious in full strength in the face of heaven.

"Woe to the presumptous one who glories in his height."

And when the winds swayed the cedar's mighty branches and his scent filled the air, the thorns turned and cried: "Woe to the presumptuous one. His pride rises like the waves of the sea. Destroy him, O Holy One in Heaven."

When the men came from the sea to put the axe to his roots they began to rejoice and say: "Thus the Lord punishes the proud, thus He humbles the mighty."

And he fell and crushed those who were rejoicing, and they were scattered among the brushwood.

And he fell crying out: "I have stood and I will stand."

And the men made him into a mast of the King's ship and the sails blew before him, and brought treasures from Ophir into the King's palace.

—J. W. Goethe

Michaelmas Song

Wind in the trees blows loud for summer's last song,
Threshing the boughs, pelting the leaves along.
Sleepers awake, hark to the word of the wind
Breaking old summer's dull drowsy spell,
Show us the way, go with thy spear before,
Forge us the future, thou Michael.

Frost on the ground at misty dawning shines bright,
Cracking the clod, lining the twigs with white.
Sleepers awake, hark to the word of the frost
Breaking old summer's dull drowsy spell,
Show us the way, go with thy spear before,
Forge us the future, thou Michael.

Myriad stars shine in the frosty clear skies,
Outshining all, the meteor earthward flies,.
Sleepers awake, hark to the word of the star
Breaking old summer's dull drowsy spell,
Show us the way, go with thy spear before,
Forge us the future, thou Michael.

With hearts aglow men mark the changing fresh world,
When from the stars Michael's spear is hurled.
Sleepers awake, hark to the word of the world
Breaking old summer's dull drowsy spell,
Show us the way, go with thy spear before,
Forge us the future, thou Michael.

—A. C. Harwood

Michael The Victorious

Thou Michael the victorious,
I make my circuit under thy shield.
Thou Michael, of the white steed
And of the bright, brilliant blade!
Conqueror of the dragon,
Be thou at my back.
Thou ranger of the heavens!
Thou warrior of the King of all!
Thou Michael the victorious
My pride and my guide!
Thou Michael the victorious
The glory of mine Eye.

—Old Gaelic

St. George

N A TIME, St. George came to the province of Libya, to a city which is said to be Silene. And by this city was a great lake wherein was a dragon which poisoned all the country. And on a time, the people were assembled to slay him, but when they saw him they fled. And when he came nigh the city he poisoned the people with his breath; and therefore the people of the city gave him every day two sheep to feed him, so that he should do no harm to the people; and when there were not enough sheep, there was taken a man and a sheep. Then was a law made in the town that there should be taken the children and young people by lot, and each one should be taken, were he gentle or simple, when the lot fell on him or her. So it happened that many of them had been taken when the lot fell upon the King's daughter, wherefore the King was sorry, and said unto the people: "Take gold and silver and all that I have, and let me have my daughter." They said, "How, Sir? Ye have made the law and our children be now dead and ye would do the contrary. Your daughter shall be given or else we shall burn you and your house."

Then the King began to weep and said to his daughter, "Now shall I never see thy marriage." Then he arrayed his daughter like as she should be wedded and kissed her and gave her his blessing and after led her to the place where the dragon was. When she was there St. George passed by on a white horse, and when he saw the lady he asked what she did there, and she said, "Go your way, fair young man, that ye perish not also." Then said he, "Tell me what is the matter and why you weep." When she saw that he would know she told him that she was delivered to the dragon. Then said St. George. "Fair daughter, I shall help thee in the name of Jesus Christ." She said, "For God's sake, young man, go your way and abide not with me, for you may not deliver me." Thus, as they spake together, the dragon appeared and came running to them; and St. George was upon his horse, and drew out his sword and made the sign of the Cross, and rode hardily against the dragon and smote him with his spear, and hurt him sore, and threw him to the ground. And St. George slew the dragon and smote off its head. Then returned they to the city, and all the people came to meet them rejoicing and the King offered to St. George as much money as there might be numbered; but he refused all and commanded that it should be given to poor people for God's sake.

—Adapted from the Golden Legend

The Ride-by-Nights

Up on their brooms the witches stream,
Crooked and black in the crescent's gleam;
One foot high and one foot low,
Bearded, cloaked, and cowled, they go.
'Neath Charlie's Wain they twitter and tweet,
And away they swarm 'neath the Dragon's feet.
With a whoop and a flutter they swing and sway,
And surge pell-mell down the Milky Way.
Betwixt the legs of the glittering Chair,
They hover and squeak in the empty air.
Then round they swoop past the glimmering
Lion to where Sirius barks behind huge Orion;
Up, then, and over to wheel amain,
Under the silver, and home again.

—Walter de la Mare

November

Golden light is turning grey,
Mists begin to rule the day,
Bare the trees their branches lift,
Clouds of dead leaves earthward drift.
Through the field the farmer goes,
Seeds of ripened corn he sows,
Trusts the earth will hold it warm,
Shelter it from cold and harm.
For he knows that warmth and light
Live there hidden from our sight,
And beneath a sheltering wing
Deep below new life will spring.

—*Elisabeth Gmeyner*

The Ploughman's Charm

Hail to thee Earth, mother of men!
Grow and be great in God's embrace,
Filled with fruit for the food of men!
Field, be full of food for men.
Blossom bright, for blessed thou art
In the name of the Holy who made the Heavens,
Created the earth on which we live,
God, who gavest us this ground,
Grant us growth and increase!
Let each seed that is sown,
Sprout and be useful.

—*Old English*

84

Our Lord and the Poor Man

THERE LIVED ONCE two farmers in a little village. They were neighbors. One of them owned a hundred sheep, the other only three. The poor man loved his three sheep, but he had not enough pasture land to feed them. So he said one day to the rich man: "Will you let my three sheep graze with your flock? I have no more pasture land, and if three more sheep are grazing on your meadow, you will hardly notice it." The rich man would rather have said no, but in the end he said yes, and the poor man's little son went out into the fields with his three sheep.

After some time the King sent to the rich farmer asking him to send a fat sheep for his table. The farmer had to fulfill the King's wish but did not want to give one of his hundred sheep away, and as he was powerful, he ordered his servants to take one of the poor man's sheep and give it to the King. And so it happened.

The little shepherd boy cried bitterly over the lost sheep. Soon there was to be another feast at the castle, and the King sent once more to the rich farmer asking for a fat sheep. Again the rich man would not take any of his hundred, and ordered that one of the poor man's sheep should be given to the King's servants.

Now the little shepherd boy cried still more, and thought to himself: "If there should be another feast and the King asked for another sheep they would take away my last one. I would rather go away with my one sheep and find pasture elsewhere."

And so he did. For a long time he wandered with his one sheep until he came to a high mountain. He went up and found a wide, rich shady meadow surrounded by high mountains, which hid and protected it from rough winds. Wonderful flowers grew there, and a clear spring flowed through the grass.

One day the poor farmer thought: "I must go and see what my boy and our three sheep are doing." When he came to the flock, he found neither the sheep nor his little son. The rich man's servants told him that he had gone off with the last remaining sheep, but where he had gone no one knew.

The poor man sadly set out to look for his son and his last sheep. He asked the way of the golden sun, but it did not know. Then he begged the wild wind to show him the way, and the wind picked him up and took him to a high mountain. From there he saw a green meadow and his son guarding his sheep. The valley was so hidden that the sun had never found it.

So he too remained in the valley as this sheep was his last possession, and they wanted to look after it together.

One day two wanderers came to their lonely dwelling and said: "We are so tired, may we spend the night with you? We also have not eaten anything for days, could you give us a little meat?" The poor man felt sorry for them, killed his sheep and fed his guests. He did not know, however, that they were Our Lord and St. Peter. When night fell Our Lord told the boy to gather up all the bones, and to put them inside the skin. The boy did this, and then they all went to bed and soon fell asleep.

Early in the morning, Our Lord and St. Peter got up very quietly, blessed the sleeping man and his son and went away.

When the poor man awoke, he looked round and saw a flock of two hundred sheep peacefully grazing. The sheep he had killed the day before, stood beside him, whole and healthy. On its forehead it carried a little disc on which was written: "All these sheep belong to the poor man and his son."

Happy and rejoicing the man gathered his flock together, and led them down to his own village. There all the people pressed round him, and everyone wanted to hear of the two strangers whom he had welcomed and fed, and who had given him this flock.

When the rich neighbor heard this, his heart was filled with envy, for his poor neighbor's sheep were more beautiful, and the flock twice as big as his own.

He therefore called together all the beggarmen and cripples, killed his whole flock, roasted the meat, and gave it to them. This, however, he did not do in order to feed the poor, but because he wanted to have still more sheep. He had all the bones collected, and put into skins. Then he went to bed already looking forward to finding twice as many sheep in the morning. But when he awoke he found no living thing. There were only the skins with the bones of the dead sheep, as on the evening before. Now he had lost everything, and remained a poor man for the rest of his life, and his neighbor who had become rich helped him as best he could.

—Russian Legend

St. Columba and the White Horse

HEN ST. COLUMBA was an old man, he looked out one morning over the island of Iona where he had lived for so long, and thought how much it had changed since he first came there from Ireland with his monks. Where had been barren rocks and heath, were now fields of corn, and among them rose up the chapel and the monastery.

Columba knew that he would soon die, and he felt he would like to make a journey through the island and speak once more to the people. So he set out in a cart, since he had not strength to walk, and visited the western fields where the brethren were working, and then he blessed the island and the islanders, and said, "When I go from you, you will have provision to last you the year."

Now the faithful Diarmid, who tended the aged man, was sorrowful, and said: "You sadden us, my father, when you talk of leaving us." Then the Saint answered: "It has been revealed to me by the Lord Himself, that this is the last day for me of this present toilsome life; at this very midnight I shall go from this earth."

Then Diarmid wept bitterly and the Saint tried to comfort him as best he could. And so they returned to the monastery, but on the way they stopped to rest, for Columba was tired from his journey and the jolting of the cart. As he sat by the roadside, there came running up the white horse that used to carry the milk pails and leaned its head against the breast of the Saint as if it were mourning. And its tears ran down its cheeks into Columba's lap.

Diarmid would have driven the creature away, but the Saint said, "Let him be, let him shed his tears of sorrow. You are a man and you did not know that I should leave you tonight, yet it has been revealed to this dumb creature that his master is to go from him."

So saying he blessed the white horse that had served him so well and it turned and went on its way.

—Legend

The Rune of St. Patrick

At Tara today in this fateful hour
I place all Heaven with its power,
And the sun with its brightness,
And the snow with its whiteness,
And the fire with all the strength it hath,
And the lightning with its rapid wrath,
And the winds with their swiftness along their path,
And the sea with its deepness,
And the rocks with their steepness,
And the earth with its starkness:
All these I place
By God's almighty help and grace,
Between myself and the powers of darkness.

—Old Gaelic

Gaelic Rune of Hospitality

I saw a stranger yesterday.
I put food in the eating place-
Drink in the drinking place-
Music in the listening place-
And in the blessed name of the Triune,
He blessed myself and my house,
My cattle and my dear ones,
And the lark said in her song:
"Often, often, often goes the Christ in the stranger's guise."

—Old Gaelic

When Days Are Darkest

When days are darkest the earth enshrines
The seeds of summer's birth.
The spirit of man is a light that shines
Deep in the darkness of earth.

—*P. S. Moffat*

Christ and St. Nicholas

CHRIST AND ST. NICHOLAS were walking on the earth. They went through many villages and towns and saw much misery, but in the fields spring flowers were blooming, God's world was beautifully adorned. On they went from house to house and Nicholas helped many men to bear their burdens; he helped everyone and refused no one. His clothes were torn and he himself began to look like a beggar.

One night as begging pilgrims, they came to a hut and asked for shelter. It was a poor hut and in it lived a soldier's widow with her children. They had no bread, only a crust and a handful of flour; there was a cow in the stable but she gave no milk.

"I have nothing to feed you with," said the woman, "not even milk. I am waiting for the cow to calve."

"Do not worry," said Christ, "we shall all have enough."

They sat down and the woman passed the crust round: it fed them all. Nicholas was even happier than the mother and children, who for once had enough to eat. Then they went to bed, but the mother went first to the cupboard. "Will there be enough flour to make a pancake for the pilgrims in the morning?" And behold, where there had just been a handful of flour, suddenly there was a whole heap!

In the morning she made pancakes for everyone. St. Nicholas was happy and how delighted were the children!

Christ was walking with St. Nicholas. They went through green cornfields; how good it was on God's earth! Nicholas thought of the harvest.

The pilgrims were tired and wished to rest, so when they saw a big farmhouse and a mill, they went up to the door. But the miller saw them and chased them away.

89

"You idlers, you beggars! You want to slip something into your pockets," he growled and threatened to let loose the dogs. So they went on.

Christ was walking with St. Nicholas. Towards evening their way led them into a wood. The wanderers lay down covered by the night and the glistening stars. Nicholas thought about the stars and the earth and could not be happy. In the middle of the night a grey wolf came into the wood, bowed before Christ and asked for food; for three days he had gone hungry.

"O Lord, I want to eat, I want to eat."

"Go, wolf, to the soldier's widow," said Christ, "her hut is at the end of the village. She has a white cow that you can eat."

"But Lord," cried Nicholas, "why that? You are taking from her the last that she has got. How the children will cry! Lord, let him take it from the miller, he chased us away and does not know where to put all his riches."

"No, it is not like that," said Christ, "her treasure is not on this earth. May she suffer till her hour is come."

But the wolf had hardly heard Christ's word when he rushed off for food. Nicholas felt cold so he got up and went to gather wood to kindle a fire. Behind the trees were the wolf's traces. Quick, after him! He overtook the wolf, who was too hungry to run fast, and reached his goal in time. He took the widow's white cow, covered her with mud and put her back in the stall; then he returned whence he had come. But now there was no need to kindle a fire, it was quite warm. The old man fell asleep. In the morning Christ wakened him. "Get up, Nicholas, it is time to go." How easily he rose! His heart was light and glad. God be praised, the wolf will take nothing and the mother need not cry. But the grey wolf came along and bowed again, "Lord, there is no white cow, only a black one."

"Take her," said Christ.

Christ was walking with St. Nicholas. Dawn was breaking, the flowers in the fields awoke and made God's world rich with color. But over there in the village, the grey wolf crept to the black cow, which was really white, killed her and ate what was his due. And when the soldier's widow came in the morning, only the horns and the bones of her white cow were left.

"God has given it, God has taken it away. His will be done." And the unhappy woman accepted her bitter lot.

The pilgrims went up the mountain. They walked silently without speaking. It was a hard road for Nicholas after the short night. Up and up went the path and when the sun arose over the world with a fiery red glow, Nicholas saw a barrel of gold rolling towards them.

"O Lord, where is this going?"

"To the miller" said Christ. "This gold is for him."

"O Lord, give at least one handful to the poor woman, she has not even the white cow left. Think of her children."

"No," said Christ, "this is how it must be; the treasure of this world is given to the miller. He shall have plenty till his hour is come."

The barrel rolled past. The path was burning hot, but the pilgrims stepped aside and the barrel rolled on till it came to the mill. The miller shovelled the gold together; among his own it was hardly noticed; one barrelful was not much.

"Oh that it were ten!" thought the miller and care sat on his shoulder.

Christ and St. Nicholas were walking upwards. Up and up, the further they went the steeper it grew. Oh if only one could rest for an hour! But they walked on and on. At the time of the evening glow they reached the summit.

"Lord, I want to drink" begged Nicholas beseechingly. "Follow this path and you will find a well. Drink there."

Nicholas went where Christ had shown him, his feet would hardly carry him. At last he found the well. He looked in to draw water, but inside snakes were writhing and he stepped back. Nearby stood the miller with bleeding hands torn by stones. "I am thirsty," he moaned, but Nicholas could not help him. He returned to Christ. "The well is not clean, Lord." Christ said nothing.

Again they went on, higher, steeper, up a still higher mountain. They were walking high above the earth, so high that they reached the stars; and the stars, so near and so stern, cut off their way.

"Lord, O Lord, I must drink!" begged Nicholas once more.

"Follow this path, there you will find a well." And Nicholas went where Christ had shown him. He dragged himself along, found the well and the water was fresh and clear. Nicholas did not recognize the place. Where were the stones? Where the precipice? How beautiful it was! Everywhere around bright light and a wonderful garden like Paradise. He stopped, looked and wondered.

The mother stood at the well, the soldier's widow. She too, stood and looked. Everything around was so wondrously beautiful and such a bright light was shining. What a Garden! Suddenly he heard a voice calling "Nicholas, Nicholas, why are you standing so long?"

"So long, Lord? Why, only three minutes have passed."

"Not three minutes, three years," said Christ.

And from the mountain they went back again to the earth.

—*Russian Legend*

Saint Christopher

THERE LIVED ONCE A MAN whose name was Offero. He was twelve feet high, strong and well built, and when he grew to his full strength, he said to himself: "I will go and seek the greatest king in all the world and be his servant." He wandered through the country, and at last he heard of a mighty king who ruled over many countries and many peoples. To him he went, and promised to serve him faithfully.

The king received him with joy; he was glad to have so strong a man; and Offero stayed with him.

One day a wandering minstrel came to the palace, and sang about many things. In his song he mentioned the name of the devil. The king turned pale, and at once made the sign of the cross.

Offero did not know this sign, and asked him what he meant by it. The king answered: "I will tell you the truth. If someone mentions the devil before me I make this sign, so that he is forced to flee, and cannot gain power over me."

Then said Offero: "If you are afraid of the devil, and if his strength is so great that it can do you harm, I will go and search till I find him, since he is more powerful than you."

Then Offero sought the devil everywhere, until one day he came into a great wilderness, where he saw many knights riding along. Among them was one who was black and ugly. Turning to Offero he said: "Whom do you seek?"

Offero answered: "I seek the devil, for I would like to be his servant."

"I am the devil," answered the black one, and Offero promised to serve him. So the devil led his servant away with him.

One day as they were riding along the road, they came to a corner where a wooden cross stood; Offero noticed how the devil took a side road to avoid passing the cross, and he said to his master: "Tell me why do you take this side road?"

The devil did not want to answer, but Offero asked again, and added: "Tell me the truth."

"I am afraid of the cross," said the devil, "because it was on such a cross that Christ once hung and I must flee from it always."

Then Offero said, "If you must flee before His sign, then He must be greater than you."

And he left the devil and would not serve him any longer.

He asked everywhere where the Lord Jesus Christ was to be found; and guided by God's will he came to a good hermit, who had heard that he wanted to serve

Christ. He told him how great and mighty a king He was and how He was the Lord of all things.

"How can I serve Him?" asked Offero.

"You must fast, and watch, and pray," said the hermit.

"I don't want to fast and watch and pray. Show me another way of serving Him," said Offero.

Then the hermit said: "There is a river over which there is no bridge. If for the sake of God you carry the people across the stream you will serve your Lord well, for you are tall and strong and can do it." "This I will gladly do," said Offero.

And he built himself a little hut by the water, and carried people across by day and by night.

One night Offero was tired, and he lay down and fell asleep. Suddenly he heard the voice of a child calling; he got up and looked out but as he could not find anyone he lay down again and slept.

But again he heard the voice calling "Offero." He ran outside and found no one.

He lay down once more, and now for the third time he heard the voice. He went out and this time he found the child. Lifting him in his arms, he took a staff in his hand, and stepped into the river.

As he did so, the water began to rise. The little child became heavier and heavier, and the water rose higher and higher, so that he was afraid he would be drowned. When he came to the middle of the river he said: "My child, how heavy you are. I feel as if I were carrying the whole world."

The child answered: "You do not only carry the world, but also Him who made Heaven and earth."

And the child pressed Offero under the water and said: "I am Jesus Christ, thy King and thy God through whom thou workest," and said unto him, "I baptize thee in the name of the Father and of Me his Son, and of the Holy Spirit. Before you were called Offero; from now onward you shall be called Christophero. Plant your staff in the earth. Through it you will behold My power, for tomorrow this dry staff will blossom and bear fruit." With these words He disappeared.

Christophero was glad and thanked the Lord for the mercy He had shown him. He planted the staff in the earth, and in one night it grew into a tree, blossomed and bore fruit. When Christophero saw this wonderful happening his heart was filled with great faith and love for God, and he thanked Him for the mercies He had shown him.

—Legend

Mary's Journey through the Stars

 UP IN THE HEAVENLY HEIGHTS, Mary is wandering from star to star, and from each one she begs a thread of golden light. She wishes to weave all these threads into a little shirt for the Christ-child when He comes down to earth.

The sun and all the glittering stars greet her, and give her of their golden rays. While the earth circles round the sun in the course of the year, Mary's way leads her from one star to another. And when men on earth celebrate their festivals, at Easter, and Whitsun, her hands are busy joining the threads, and weaving them into a soft shimmering web.

She has to make haste for at Christmas the little shirt must be finished, and often she wonders if she will really achieve it, for stargold alone will not hold together; again and again the beautifully set threads fall apart. But the angels of the children on earth come to help her. They carry up to her the children's good deeds, thoughts and words. Up there these are all changed into gold. Softly it shines through the shimmering threads.

And Mary joins the threads of earthly gold with the threads of heavenly gold, and of both together she prepares the Christ-child's radiant garment for Christmas.

All children can help her.

Over stars is Mary wandering;
In her mantle's flowing folds,
Radiant threads of starlight woven
For her little Child she holds.
Throngs of stars behold her passing,
All the sky is filled with light,
With her hands she weaves and gathers
Blessings for the Christmas night.

—*After Karl Schubert*

The Legend of St. Bridget

THE ISLAND OF IONA lies in the western seas; and whoever has felt the breath of the wind and the kiss of the light above those lonely hills, knows that it is a holy place. For these shores were the haunt of St. Bridget, the foster-mother of the King of the World.

Dughall, Prince of Ireland, was driven from his native land. It was said that he had married a maiden against his father's will and that the child Bridget was his; but now it is known that no mortal father could claim that babe. The King was wroth and believed ill of his son, so Dughall and Bridget were placed in a tiny boat and set afloat on the wild waves. Surely no power could bring their frail craft to land. The clouds gathered and the wind rose. Lightning flashed across the dark sky. Dughall held the babe in his arms so that they should die together. But suddenly it seemed as though sunlight pierced the clouds and there in the glory of golden light shone a child with a face so gentle and mild that Dughall bowed his head. The child stretched forth her hands and lo! the wind sank and the waves were stilled. It seemed then to Dughall that the waters murmured, "O King of the Elements, we are thy servants and thy command shall be obeyed."

A light breeze caught the frail boat and carried it gently through the waves to a quiet cove Then the little maid who had not yet stood or walked stepped on to the beach and spoke words which Dughall did not understand.

"I am but a little child, yet these arms shall enfold the Lord of the World. The King of the Elements himself shall rest on my heart."

A white-robed priest came down to welcome the wanderers. He told them that they had been guided to the holy island of Iona where every dawn the sacred fire was kindled to greet the rising sun. From day to day the priests kept watch for they said that soon on earth a holy child was to be born who would be King of the Elements, and they would surely see the signs of his approach.

For many years Dughall and Bridget lived on the island and the priests taught the young maid their holy lore. They welcomed her where no unhallowed foot might tread and she stood with them before the altar to greet the morning light.

It was Bridget's birthday and the island slumbered in the warm spring light. Robed in white she wandered over the hill to a place she loved to sit and dream. There between the rowan trees lay the mountain pool known as the Fountain of Youth. The trees were green with their first leaves and the waters reflected the ever changing light of sun and cloud. Bridget leaned over to drink the cool water and gazed into the still depths. But as she gazed she saw in wonder that behind the image of her own form there gleamed, not the wide blue sky and the passing clouds, but a beautiful woman standing with arms outspread as though in blessing. Above her the trees were no longer green as in early spring but they twined their branches to form a crown, bright with scarlet berries. The woman's gown was redder than the rowans and her outspread robe, shining with stars, a deeper blue than the midday sky. Bridget turned to see who stood behind her but no one was there, she was alone under the wide heavens. Then a longing rose in her heart to seek this beautiful stranger but she did not know what path to follow.

A white thrush began to sing among the rowan trees and a dove flew down before her as though it wished to guide her on her way. Bridget followed until twilight spread its wings over the earth and from far away a golden star shed its guiding ray. Onward through mist and cloud, through water and light lay the path of Bridget and when storms swept over the ocean, it seemed as though helping hands held her aloft and when the way led her through desert wastes, unseen powers nourished and supported her.

At last she found herself in a strange land where the trees were unknown to her and where the people spoke a foreign tongue. The earth was dry and hard as though with drought, the plants had withered and died and the animals drooped for lack of water. Ahead of her lay a little village and among the houses clustering together on the mountain slope she saw a white inn. As she drew near, the landlord came to meet her and she saw that he was none other than her foster-father Dughall.

He showed no surprise but he said, "Guard my inn until my return. I go to seek for water from the Mount of Olives for there has been no rain and all the springs are dry. Promise me that you will admit no more guests for the inn is full and there is barely a morsel of food or a drop of ale left in the house."

Bridget took charge of the inn and for three days no rain fell and no drop of moisture came to bless the ground. The ale was almost gone and the water barrel was empty when on the third day she heard a knock on the door. Outside there stood an old man, bent with age, leading a donkey, and on its back was seated a beautiful woman. "Pray give us shelter for the night" said the old man. "We have travelled far and Mary my wife is weary."

She gazed at the woman sitting upon the ass and when she saw those deep dark eyes, memory stirred in her heart. "The landlord has given me orders that no more guests be brought to the inn," said Bridget "for it is already crowded and there is no drink to spare."

"O Bridget, do you not remember me?" said the woman. "Who was it that gazed into your eyes by the mountain pool? Look into your heart and remember."

"It was you who stood beside me at the mountain pool," said Bridget, "and your mantle of stars embraced the whole wide world. I may not admit you to the inn, but there is a stable which will shelter you from the cold and where you may rest and I will bring you whatever food is left."

Bridget led the old man and his wife to the stable and brought them bread and ale. Yet when she returned to the inn she saw that the loaf of bread was untouched and the flagon of ale was full.

Late at night Dughall returned from the Mount of Olives with his cruse full of water. Bridget began to tell him of the strange travellers but he cried to her to be silent and listen. There could be heard the sound of quiet rain falling upon the earth, yet above, the sky was blue and cloudless.

"There is an old saying," said Dughall, "that when after long drought the rain falls from a cloudless heaven, the Lord of all the World will come to earth. Let us seek these strange travellers."

Bridget and her foster-father softly opened the door of the stable. So bright was the light shining through the dark abode that it seemed as though the sun himself had come to dwell therein. Between the ox and the ass sat the young mother with her child upon her knee and Joseph kneeled before them in wonder and in love. "Who is this child?" Dughall whispered in awe.

"The Prince of Peace." said Joseph.

Mary held out the little one to Bridget. "Bridget, my sister, this night you shall be His nurse that I may sleep."

The maiden took the child and folding Him in her mantle, lulled Him on her heart until He slept.

Far away in Iona the Arch Druid Cathal was dying. But e'er he closed his eyes there dawned upon them the vision of Bridget with the King of the Elements sleeping on her breast and he smiled for joy that this sight had been granted him before his death. In the morning Mary took the child once more, and bending over Bridget she kissed her softly with the words.

"From now through all eternity you shall be known as my sister, the foster-mother of the Holy Child."

Bridget fell into a deep slumber and when she awoke late in the day, the stable was empty and the Mother and Child nowhere to be seen.

Was it all a strange and beautiful dream? Yet when she looked at the cloak wherein she had wrapped the King of the World, it was bright with stars.

She longed to find the Mother and Child once more, and passing out on to the hillside, she looked for a sign to show the way they had gone. And lo! before her in the moonlight she saw the footsteps of a woman shining in the dew. With love and wonder Bride followed those steps, for she knew that the King of the Elements was her guide.

Day dawned and the footsteps were no longer to be seen. But she heard the cry of a seabird and before her lay a gleaming pool fringed with rowan trees. She stood once more on the hills of Iona and the murmuring of the sea was in her ears. The Foster-Mother of the Prince of Peace had returned to the waiting Druids with the words for which they longed, "Behold! the King of the Elements has come to birth!"

The Date Palm

WHEN MARY AND JOSEPH fled from Bethlehem to save the Child Jesus from the wrath of Herod, they had to pass through a desert land. The hot sun shone down upon them and they had no water to quench their thirst.

After a time they came to a tall date palm and sat down to rest in its shade. Far above them they could see the clusters of fruit among the leaves, but they were out of reach.

Then the palm bowed its tall trunk till Mary and Joseph could pluck the dates with ease and at the same moment a spring of fresh water gushed forth from its roots. Thus were they able to drink of the sweet waters and continued on their way refreshed.

—From an Apocryphal Gospel

As Joseph Was A-Walking

As Joseph was a-walking,
He heard an angel sing:
"This night there shall be born
On earth our heavenly king;

He neither shall be born
In housen nor in hall,
Nor in the place of Paradise,
But in an ox's stall.

He neither shall be clothed
In purple nor in pall,
But all in fair linen
As wear the babies all.

He neither shall be rocked
In silver nor in gold
But in a wooden cradle
That rocks upon the mould.

He neither shall be christened
In white wine nor red,
But with fair spring water
As we were christened."

—*Carol*

I Sing of a Maiden

I sing of a maiden
That is makeless,
King of all Kings
To her son she ches.

He came all so still
Where his mother was,
As dew in April
That falleth on the grass.

He came all so still
To his mother's bower,
As dew in April
That falleth on the flower.

He came all so still
Where his mother lay,
As dew in April
That falleth on the spray.

Mother and maiden
Was never none but she;
Well may such a lady
God's mother be.

—Carol

New Year Carol

Here we bring new water
From the well so clear,
For to worship God with
This happy New Year.
Sing levy dew, sing levy dew,
The water and the wine;
The seven bright gold wires
And the bugles that do shine.

Sing reign of Fair Maid
With gold upon her toe,
Open you the West Door
And let the Old Year go.

Sing reign of Fair Maid
With gold upon her chin—
Open you the East Door
And let the New Year in.
Sing levy dew, sing levy dew,
The water and the wine;
The seven bright gold wires
And the bugles that do shine.

—*Old English*

The Ball of Crystal and the Saucer of Silver

NCE UPON A TIME there lived a man who had three daughters. The eldest one was proud and the second was greedy but the youngest was as fair as the day and was the apple of her Father's eye. One day he had to go to the fair. "What shall I bring you, my daughters? "

"Bring me a scarlet robe," said the eldest.

"Bring me a necklace of shining stones," said the second.

"And what for you, my little one?"

"O Father, I do not need a present. You love me, and that is enough." "But I should like to bring you a gift from the fair."

"Then bring me a ball of crystal and a saucer of silver."

The Father went to the fair and he soon found a beautiful scarlet dress and a necklace of shining green stones, but nowhere, nowhere in all the fair, could he find a ball of crystal and a saucer of silver. He searched all day. At last evening came and the stall holders were packing away their goods and one by one riding away to their homes. At last the Father saw a little old man with a tiny stall hidden away in a quiet corner.

"What can I do for you, good sir?" "I do not think you can help me. I am searching everywhere for a ball of crystal and a saucer of silver, but there are none to be found in the fair."

"I have a ball of crystal and a saucer of silver," said the little old man. The Father nearly danced for joy.

"What do I owe you, good friend?"

"You owe me nothing. If it is rightly used that is reward enough for me." The Father journeyed home as quickly as his good steed could carry him. The elder daughters were watching from the window and as soon as they saw him come riding up the road they ran to meet him.

"Father, have you my scarlet dress?"

"Here is your scarlet dress, my daughter."

"Father, have you my shining beads? "

"Here are your shining beads, my child."

Presently the youngest daughter came.

"Dear Father, how tired you must be, but the fire burns brightly and the soup is hot. Come and refresh yourself." The Father kissed his dear daughter and gave her the ball of crystal and the saucer of silver, but she put it away until she had seen that he was rested and refreshed.

At last she crept away by herself into a corner.

"What is our sister doing?" said the two elder ones. "Whoever heard of such a foolish present as a ball of crystal and a saucer of silver. Let us go and see what she is doing."

Unheard they crept up behind her.

The youngest sister took the ball of crystal and laying it in the saucer of silver, she spoke these words:

"Roll, roll, little ball in my saucer of silver and show me the cities of the world."

The ball rolled and soon it began to shine till in the shimmering crystal, pictures slowly came into view. There appeared walls and turrets and gleaming domes, and towering above them all the golden palace of the Czar. The picture glowed, grew bright and clear and then began to fade.

She spoke again, "Roll, roll, little ball in my saucer of silver and show me the oceans and seas."

The ball rolled and again shining pictures began to appear. The sisters could see the waves of the ocean and the wide waters bearing countless fleets of ships. The picture glowed, grew bright and then began to fade.

She spoke a third time, "Roll, roll, little ball, in my saucer of silver and show me the heavens, with the sun, the moon and the stars in all their glory."

Then the ball began to roll a third time, and from amid the shining crystal they saw the fires of the heavens, the moon and the stars and the sun in its splendour.

Then the sisters were seized with longing for this beautiful treasure. They came to the youngest daughter.

"Sister, give me your present and you shall have my scarlet dress."

"Sister, give me your ball of crystal and your saucer of silver and you shall have my bright green beads."

But the youngest daughter replied: "This is my Father's present, I cannot give it away."

Then the wicked sisters were mad with jealousy and anger, and they thought that if they could not get hold of it one way they would get hold of it another.

One day the sun was shining brightly and the forest was gay with all its summer blossoms.

"Sister, sister, come with us, we go to gather strawberries."

The youngest daughter went with them far into the forest.

"Is it not time to return, our Father will be seeking his supper?"

"Nonsense! The day is yet young."

Further and further they wandered into the wood.

"Should we not turn back? Evening is already falling and our Father will be anxious."

"How ridiculous! We have gathered nothing, we cannot return yet."

They came to a woodland glade, where the trees stood aside and where the grass was bright and long. Someone had been digging for water and had left a spade.

"Look, sister, down among the grass there are strawberries. Gather them quickly and then we can return."

The youngest daughter bent to look among the grass, and as she stooped the two elder ones came behind and struck her with the spade. They killed her and buried her under the green ground. Then they returned to their Father.

They said that their youngest sister had foolishly wandered away into the woods and the wolves must have seized her. The Father searched everywhere but she was nowhere to be found and he grieved and mourned for his lost daughter.

The two sisters hurried to the place where the saucer of silver and the ball of crystal had been left.

"Roll, roll, little ball, in my saucer of silver and show me the cities of the world."

But the ball was still and silent, it made no movement and no pictures gleamed or glowed in its clear crystal. Again and again they tried to persuade it to work but it always remained motionless so at last disappointed and angry they gave up the attempt.

Spring returned to the forest and one day a shepherd boy was wandering through the woodland in search of a hollow reed to make a pipe. At last he came to a sunny opening where the trees stood aside and the grass was long and green. There in the heart of the glade grew flowers of blue and red and white and above them the wind murmured among the bulrushes. The shepherd boy cut one of the rushes and shaping it into a pipe he started to play. But the music he tried to flute seemed to blow away in the empty air and instead the pipe began to sing its own song. Wonderfully strange and sad were the notes of that music and soon words began to form:

O sing unto the world my song,
The woeful song of how I died.
My sisters did me grievous wrong
And laid me in the cold woodside.

The shepherd boy wandered on his way entranced. He came to a village and as he passed through the streets the sweet voice continued:

And where the flowers are white and red
I lie and wait below the clay
For one to wake me from the dead
And lead me to the light of day.

The Father came rushing out of his house. "That is the voice of my lost child. Shepherd boy, where did you learn that song?"

The shepherd led him to the glade in the forest. And where the flowers blossomed blue and white and red and where the wind hummed in the bulrushes, they found the old spade and they dug below the ground.

As they turned the grass aside, there lay the maiden as though asleep, and if she were lovely before, she was now dazzlingly beautiful.

The Father wept for the death of his daughter, but the shepherd boy cried, "Do not grieve! In the palace of the Czar flows the fountain of the water of life. I will seek from him three holy drops to rouse her from the dead."

The shepherd boy went to the Czar but the servants would not admit him; he was too poor and lowly. Then he put his pipe to his lips and it sang once more the story of the maid who was slain.

The Czar in his palace heard the sad refrain. "Who is singing that strange sweet song?" "It is only a poor shepherd boy, Your Majesty." "Bring him to me."

The shepherd boy was led before the Czar and falling on his knees before him begged for three drops of the water of life. The Czar went to the fountain and bade the spirit of the well pour forth her waters:

Water of life,
O fountain head,
Weep thy tears
For a maiden dead.
Water of life,
O quickening stream,
Rouse a maid
From her winter dream.

Then the spirit caused the water to well forth for him, and with three drops from its living stream he sought the maiden. He touched her head, her heart and her hands and she stood before them shining in light.

The Czar asked to see her ball of crystal and her saucer of silver and when he had beheld the cities with their towers, the wide seas with their fleets and the sun, moon and stars in their glory, he cried "Beautiful maiden, you alone are worthy to be my bride. Your cruel sisters shall be slain and you and your father shall come to my palace and live with me in joy."

But the beautiful maiden pleaded for her sisters' lives. They had suffered enough already, for the ball of crystal and the saucer of silver would not reveal to them its secrets. Then the Czar turned to the shepherd and offered him a rich reward. But the shepherd replied:

"Your Majesty, I am a poor shepherd boy and I would rather wander in the woods and pipe sweet songs than live in the palaces of Kings. But every year when the Spring is bright in the woodland, I will pass below your turrets and greet you with my loveliest songs of joy."

The shepherd was allowed his wish and then with one accord they all made merry for it was the joyful wedding day of the Czar and his bride.

—Russian Fairy Tale

Bashtchelik (True Steel)

THE OLD CZAR LAY DYING. He called around him his three sons and his three daughters to leave with them his last earthly bequests. "O my sons," he said, "to you I leave my kingdom. Love one another and rule justly. But I give you one last command before I die. Whoever may come to seek your sisters in marriage, grant your permission freely. If you do not act as I say, a terrible punishment will fall upon you for having disobeyed my last earthly wish."

Then the old Czar closed his eyes and his soul left the earth, which he had ruled for so long. The three brothers and the three sisters sat beside him to keep watch, for they now felt very sad and lonely.

Suddenly they were disturbed by a great storm which seemed to sweep up the valley. The walls shook, the doors rattled and the wind howled around the castle turrets. While the sisters and brothers clung together in fear, there was a flash of lightning followed by a mighty roll of thunder and a voice called out of the night.

"In the name of the King, open the gates! I have come to claim your eldest sister in marriage."

"That is impossible!" said the eldest son.

"Whoever heard of a princess marrying a thunderstorm?" said the second. "Remember the dying command of our Father," said the youngest. "What have we to fear? I will open the gates."

The Prince took his eldest sister by the hand and led her through the palace courtyard. He opened the great gates and looked out into the storm. No one was there, but a flash of lightning suddenly lit up the darkness and the princess seemed to be lifted from his side and caught up into the clouds. At the same moment the gates clashed together and a loud roll of thunder shook the firmament.

The courtiers fell on their knees for fear and prayed that they might be spared from the wrath of heaven, while the prince returned to the castle alone. The second night the brothers and sisters were again keeping watch, when once more a violent tempest came sweeping round the castle; it blew in gusts down the chimneys, whistled below the doors, and billowed the curtains out into the room.

It seemed as though the winds were raging from all the quarters of the earth at once, each one trying to out-roar the other. From the midst of the blast a great voice was heard crying: "Open the gates in the King's name! I have come to claim your second sister in marriage."

"That is impossible!" said the eldest brother. "Remember what happened last night."

"Impossible indeed," cried the second. "Whoever heard of a King's daughter marrying a whirlwind?"

"Have you forgotten our Father's last command?" said the youngest. "Though the heavens threaten us, I will obey him and open the gates."

Taking his second sister by the hand, the prince led her across the courtyard and opened the massive gates. They looked out but there was no one to be seen. All the winds of heaven seemed to be warring together and the clouds were torn into fragments and whirled about the castle in ever changing forms. Suddenly a passing gust swept the princess from his side. Away, away she went with the racing clouds and was lost in the darkness of the night. All the courtiers held their breath for fear and hid behind the curtains and the hangings, while the prince returned sadly to his brothers and sister.

The third night was still more terrible to endure. The heavens were silent and no wind could be heard but the earth shook and every turret of the castle began to tremble. The brothers and sister did not dare to move for at any moment the palace might crash upon their heads. The very foundations of the earth seemed to rock. Then from the rumbling of the deep came a mighty voice. "I have come to claim in marriage the hand of your youngest sister."

"We have already lost two sisters," said the eldest brother, "and I refuse to allow our youngest and dearest one to leave us."

"It was wrong to allow the lightning and the whirlwind to claim our sisters," said the second, "but to give our last one to an earthquake would be a crime."

"Do you so little value the promise you gave our Father?" said the youngest son. "Terrible punishment falls on those who disobey the wishes of the dying. But it is not for fear of punishment but because I loved our Father that I wish to carry out his last command. I will open the gates and give my sister to this strange suitor."

The youngest brother took his sister's hand and led her out through the night. He opened the gates of the castle but there was no one to be seen, for all was dark. Suddenly the earth trembled and everything around him seemed to reel and sway. The prince turned to his sister to protect her, but she was gone. He was standing all alone outside the castle gates.

Within the castle the princes and all the courtiers had fallen upon their faces for fear, for it seemed to them that the end of the earth had come.

The two eldest brothers mourned and grieved for their sisters, saying that they were lost for ever, but the youngest one consoled them.

"Dear brothers," said he, "have we not obeyed our Father's dying wish, and shall we not on that account be blessed? How can our sisters be lost? Somewhere in the world they are bound to be. Let us go forth and seek them."

At this the brothers took courage and all three set out into the world to seek their sisters. They journeyed on and on through field and wood, over hill and mountain, by lake and stream until all human habitation was left behind and they came to a great forest. All day they travelled beneath dark overhanging trees and saw no sign of life until at last at evening time they reached a great lake.

"Let us rest here," said the eldest brother, "and as it seems a wild and unfriendly spot, one of us had better keep watch, for who knows what wild beasts or robbers may not be prowling around in quest of prey. I am the eldest, I will watch tonight."

The other two (wrapped in their cloaks) lay down by the shore of the lake and soon they were sound asleep. But the eldest brother kept watch. He listened with all his ears to make sure that no enemy was at hand. Far, far away he heard the bark of a fox, and then from some distant ivy-covered tree an owl began to hoot, but soon the fox and the owl were silent and all was still as stone. There was not a sound in the wide world.

Then it seemed to the eldest brother that the water of the lake began to stir, and slowly above the ripples there rose a black head. Nearer and nearer it drew to the shore. As the head reared itself aloft and opened its great jaws with gleaming fangs, the prince saw that it was a huge monster coming to devour him. He was a brave warrior and undaunted he drew his sword to attack the terrible creature. Down, down it came, its great jaws gaping wide, its eyes gleaming with greed and malice. Flash! went the prince's sword like a streak of lightning and the black head fell severed from the body.

The uncouth headless creature sank back into the waters of the lake, while the prince leapt forward and cut off the two great ears. He put these carefully in his pouch. Then he pushed the head back into the lake where it disappeared below the surface.

The grey dawn was beginning to shine over the hills when the prince roused his brothers. "Have you had a quiet watch?" they asked. "Very quiet," answered the eldest prince, and he said not a word of his strange adventure.

All the next day they journeyed on again through wild and gloomy forests until at nightfall they reached another lake.

"Here let us rest," said the second brother, "and tonight it is my turn to keep guard."

The others lay down on the ground, wrapped in their mantles, and were soon sound asleep.

The second brother listened intently. He expected to hear the howl of wolves or the sound of a lion prowling in search of prey, but there was only the gentle stirring of the wind in the reeds and the lapping of the water on the shore. Bye and bye the evening breeze died away and soon even the waves and the rushes seemed to sleep. The night was still as death; he could hear not a sound. Then it seemed to him that the surface of the lake began to tremble. Slowly there rose two great dark heads above the surface. It was a terrible monster with gaping jaws which every moment drew nearer to devour him.

The prince leapt to the side and drew his sword. Flash, went the prince's bright blade and one of the heads fell to the ground. Flash, flash, and the second was severed from the body, which sank slowly back into the lake. The prince sprang forward and cut the ears from the two heads, then he rolled them into the water where they disappeared.

At last the grey dawn came over the eastern hills and the brothers awoke.

"Did you have a quiet watch?" they asked. "Not a sound to be heard," replied the prince, for he had decided not to speak a word of what had happened during the night.

All day they travelled on again through dark immeasurable forests and when night was falling they came to a third lake.

"Tonight it is my turn to watch," said the youngest prince.

Within this lake there lived a far more terrible monster than the ones his brothers had encountered, and when all was still, at the hour of midnight, the waters of the lake began to stir. Above the waves there rose a gigantic creature with three heads and it rapidly drew near to the shore as though seeking to devour all the brothers in one great gulp. The youngest prince drew his sword. Flash to the right, flash to the left, flash, flash, upward and downward; and lo and behold! the three heads lay severed from the monstrous body. The lake sucked back the giant form, while the prince leapt forward and cut off the six ears which he carefully placed in his pouch. Then he flung the heads back into the lake and turned to greet his brothers. It was still dark and they were slumbering peacefully, but the prince was cold and decided that he would kindle a fire so he set out to look for sticks. He wandered here and there gathering a few dry twigs, when far in the distance he saw a gleam of light. "That is surely some shepherd's fire," thought he. "I will go and beg from them a glowing ember."

He made his way over rocks and stones until he found himself standing outside a cave. The prince nearly cried aloud in astonishment, for there, inside, seated in a circle and feasting off human bones, sat nine great giants.

But the prince knew that whatever happened he must show no fear, so boldly stepping into their midst he cried out, "Good morning, good brothers! You are the very people whom I have been seeking."

The giants looked at him in surprise, but he spoke so boldly and looked at them with such confidence that they thought he must certainly be a friend.

"Good morning, little one," said their leader. "We do not know you, but you seem to be one of our kind. Come and show your good fellowship by feasting with us."

The prince sat down in their circle and they started passing to him portions of their grisly feast; but with great skill he pretended to eat while in reality he dropped the bones behind him. All the while he talked so freely and boasted so loudly about his many exploits that the giants did not notice what he was doing.

"And what is your name, O valiant sir?" said the leader, "I am called Nine Man Mord," replied the prince, giving the name of a hero who had made himself famous by slaying nine enemies with one stroke.

"We have heard of his mighty deeds," said the giants, "and we are indeed lucky to have so sturdy a fellow among us. Come now, it is time to go hunting."

They all made their way out of the cave and the chief giant led the way. "Not far from here," he said, "there is a big town where we will find plenty to eat."

They soon reached the walls of a city and the giants began to make preparations for climbing over by pulling up two great trees and leaning one of them against the ramparts. Then the leader called out, "Nine Man Mord, as you are the lightest, you shall climb to the top first and fasten the trees so that all will be safe for us to climb over."

The prince climbed the tree and then the giants pushed up the second for him to fix as a ladder on the other side.

"All is ready," cried the prince. One by one the giants climbed to the top, crossed the wall and began to descend the tree on the other side. But just as each one was safely out of sight of the others down below, the prince drew his sword and smote off the giant's head.

He cried to the next, "Come up quickly, your companion is safely over." All in turn climbed over and quick was their descent. Last of all came the leader. He paused for a moment at the top of the wall. "What are they doing?" he cried. But before he had time to see what lay at the bottom of the tree, the prince had severed his head from his body and down he went to the bottom at the fastest possible speed.

Sheathing his sword, the prince climbed down and passing the nine headless bodies he began to explore the city. All the streets were dark and deserted and the houses looked as though they were falling into decay. For many months now the giants had been coming night after night in search of prey, so that at last the Czar had issued a command that as soon as the sun set, all lights were to be quenched, all doors locked and no one was to pass through the streets of the city. Thus the prince in his wandering did not meet a single soul.

Strange to say, after a while he saw a distant light shining from a turret window.

"Here at least," thought the prince, "is some lonely soul who is keeping watch." He made his way in that direction and soon came to a tower with a small postern door, which was standing ajar. The prince pushed it open and made his way up a flight of winding stairs.

At the top was a door leading into a turret room whence shone the rays of the light. The prince entered and gazed entranced, for on a stately bed of gold lay the most beautiful maiden he had ever seen. Her hair outshone the gold in its glory and her skin was whiter than the purest snow. But as he gazed he saw that there was another watcher in that room. Above the bed there hung a terrible serpent with cold glittering eyes, its neck arched and its fangs ready to strike as soon as the sleeper gave the faintest stir of life. With a cry, the prince drew his dagger. "Hold wood, hold dagger!" he cried. "May only the true owner draw forth this blade from the wood." With one swift stroke he pierced the neck of the serpent, leaving it pinned securely to the wall.

He then left the tower and passing swiftly through the deserted street, climbed back over the tree ladder to join his brothers beside the lake. They were still sleeping. As the dawn was beginning to peep over the Eastern hills he roused them from their slumber.

"Did you have a quiet watch?" they asked.

"Very peaceful," replied the youngest brother, for he also had decided not to say anything about the strange adventures of the night.

"However," he added, "I took a little stroll just before the dawn and not far away I saw the walls of a city, so I suggest that we set out together to seek some food and lodging."

The brothers readily agreed for they were becoming weary of their long travels in wild forests, and their cold nights' rest.

Before long they were all comfortably seated in a warm inn enjoying a hearty meal and drinking one another's health in good red wine. Their striking and handsome appearance soon attracted the attention of a stranger who was sitting by the fire. As the three young princes were friendly and talkative, conversation began to flow and after recounting some of his most daring deeds, the stranger said, "But now, young men, I am sure you have a good number of exploits to your names."

The eldest prince replied, "We are young and have not yet seen a great deal of the world, but three nights ago I did have an adventure. I was attacked by a great monster which I promptly slew, and to witness the truth of my statement, here are its ears." He opened his pouch and threw on the table the two ears of the creature he had killed.

"Bless me!" said the second, "I have also slain a monster, but it had two heads," and he produced the four ears.

"The dragon that attacked me," said the youngest, "had three heads, and here are the six ears."

All of them gazed at the youngest brother in astonishment for it had never occurred to them that he could do the bravest deed.

"You are indeed valiant," said the stranger. "I should think you are almost as strong as the unknown hero who visited the city during the night. You must know that for many months the town has been attacked by terrible giants, so that most of our flocks and herds have been destroyed and many people have lost their lives.

Every night a few more disappeared from their homes. But this morning when the Czar took his daily walk through the city to see how his subjects were faring, what do you think he saw? There, under the wall lay all the giants with their heads severed from their bodies.

But this was not the only wonder that befell during the night. When he came to the room of his daughter, the princess, she was slumbering sweetly, while above her head, pinned to the wall by a dagger, hung a terrible serpent which must have been slain just as it was about to destroy her. The dagger still stands fixed in the wall and the Czar has offered his daughter's hand in marriage to the one who can withdraw it, for he must be the true slayer of the serpent."

The young prince now confessed that he was none other than the destroyer of the giants and the snake.

"Come at once to the Czar," said the stranger,."If you are indeed as you say, you will be able to pull forth the dagger and prove your right to the hand of the princess."

Accompanied by the stranger, the three brothers at once hastened to the tower room which was already crowded with the King's courtiers, all trying to lay their claim to the dagger. But none could move it.

The Czar at first doubted the prince's story and asked all three brothers to try their strength. The eldest brother clasped the handle of the dagger and pulled with all his might, but it refused to move even the fraction of an inch. The second brother was equally unsuccessful. Then the third seized it.

"Yield wood! Yield dagger! The true owner draws forth the blade," he cried.

With one wrench he drew the dagger from the wall and the snake fell to the floor. All around proclaimed him the hero who had saved their city from the giants and their princess from the serpent, and the Czar fulfilled his promise of uniting him to the princess.

For a while all was joy. The wedding bells rang, everyone feasted and danced and life seemed to be one gay song. But at last the festivities were over and the city was quiet once more. The Czar offered the two elder princes castles and land if they would like to settle in his kingdom, but they still mourned for their three sisters and decided to set out again on their search. The youngest son, however, stayed with his wife, the princess.

As he loved her dearly he was at first very happy, but bye and bye he began to reproach himself for being contented and idle when his brothers were enduring toil and hardship and his three sisters had not been found. From day to day he grew more and more sad and melancholy. The old Czar could not fail to observe this and he tried in every way to cheer his son-in-law and help him to forget his sorrow.

One day the Czar said: "My son, to-day I go forth to hunt, but as I see that you no longer enjoy the pleasures of the chase, I will ask you to guard my palace until my return. Here are the nine keys of my secret chambers. They contain many beauties which I hope will bring you delight, for the first four rooms reveal the joys of Earth; the next three unfold the joys of Heaven, and the eighth contains the joys of Earth and Heaven in one. But into the ninth room you must not go or great misfortune will befall us."

The Czar set off on the hunt and the Prince began to explore. One by one he opened the secret rooms. In the first he saw the wonders of the rocks and the stones, the shining jewels and the veins of gold and silver that hide in the heart of the earth. In the second he beheld the beauty of the flowers and trees, the joy of the first leaves that unfold in the spring and the glory of the meadows bright with blossom and fruit. The third room showed him the strength and grace of the animal world, the swift eagle, the mighty lion and the darting fish; while in the fourth he was confronted with all that man has attained in building and shaping the earth to his mind. But greater glories were to come. The fifth room revealed to him the beauty of the sun, in the sixth he entered the realm of the moon, and in the seventh he found himself in the wide spaces where the countless stars have made their home. Glorious and great were these kingdoms, but in the eighth room all joys were united for he saw the beauty of Heaven and Earth in one, the air was full of wonderful music, and words cannot describe the light and joy that filled his heart.

At last he stood before the door of the ninth. "What can be within this room that I am not worthy to behold?" he asked himself. "Have I not slain the three-headed monster? Have I not saved the life of the princess? This is a test which the Czar has set. I must now show him that I am undaunted and can dare all."

The prince turned the key and entered the room. But here no glory met his eyes. He was in a dark vault, and near him bound to a pillar stood a tall figure. It seemed to have the strength of the underworld in its limbs, of the mid-world in its set face and of the heavens in its proud defiant gaze. It was held captive with all the metals of the earth.

Chains of gold encircled its breast; its limbs were bound in fetters of iron, a silver band secured its head to the pillar; and a girdle of copper entwined its waist and was fixed to the stone of the wall. Far away through distant windows, remote and unattainable, the captive could behold the joys of the other rooms.

"Young man, for the love of Heaven," said the strange being, "bring me a drink of water from yonder fountain. For many a long year have I languished in these chains and not one drop has passed my lips."

The prince hesitated for he had been forbidden to enter this chamber and was doubtful whether he ought to commit any further act.

But the creature cried, "Only one draught of water, and I will give thee a priceless reward. When thy time comes to die I will grant thee a second life."

A second life seemed to the prince a very desirable gift, so he hastened to the fountain and returned with a bowl of water.

The creature drank it at one draught and seemed to grow taller and straighter. "What is your name?" said the prince.

"Bashtchelik, which meaneth True Steel," was the reply. "But O Prince, one bowl of water is but little for so great and strong a being as I. Bring me one more bowl I pray thee and I will grant thee yet another life."

A bowl of water was a small payment for another life, so the prince hastened to the fountain and gave Bashtchelik a second drink. It seemed that the strange being grew still taller and mightier.

But now the prince could hear the sounds of the Czar and his company returning from the chase, and fearing to be found in his act of disobedience he turned to hurry away.

"Farewell!" he cried, "The Czar returns and I must go."

"O noble prince," continued Bashtchelik, "I know thee, I have heard of thy brave deeds. Truly there is none like thee. Give me but one more drink and I will give thee a third life, for thou art worthy."

The prince could not resist the promise of yet another life for so small a cost. He hastened to the fountain for the third drink, but even as he brought it the Czar could be heard at the gates. As Bashtchelik took the drink he and the prince gazed at one another, and the prince had never known a glance so compelling as that proud gaze. It seemed to him that the strange being grew every moment taller and stronger. Suddenly there was the sound of the rending of chains; the fetters fell apart; Bashtchelik stretched himself, and lo and behold mighty wings were outspread from his shoulders. In one flash he was out of the door, he had swept through the passage, and leapt across the terrace. In front of the palace the princess was enjoying the evening air. In full sight of the Czar returning from the chase, Bashtchelik caught the princess into his arms and soared away over the clouds beyond their furthest sight.

"Alas!" cried the Czar, "What have you done? I lost three armies in capturing this terrible being and now that he goes forth with renewed strength, he will never be taken prisoner again."

"Do not despair," said the prince, "I will not rest until I have found Bashtchelik and won back my bride."

"God be with you," said the Czar, "for it is a hopeless quest."

Nothing daunted the prince set forth. Everywhere seeking for news of Bashtchelik, he rode through many strange lands until one day he came to a beautiful city. Strange to say, it seemed to be empty, but as he rode through the deserted streets under the great strong walls, he heard a voice calling him. In answer he dismounted and turned to enter the courtyard, when a girl came running out to meet him. With great joy, the prince clasped her in his arms, for it was none other than his eldest sister.

"How do you come to be here?" he asked at length. "This is the city where I am Queen," she replied, "my husband is the Falcon King; but all day long he is far away with his army of falcons and we can enjoy each other's company. When he returns I must hide you for he does not love my brothers."

She led him to a high tower and gave him food and drink more delicious than any he had tasted on his long journeys. They had so much to tell each other that the day soon passed. As evening came the air was filled with the whirring of wings.

Presently the Falcon King came sweeping into his palace chamber, but there was no sign of the prince or his gallant horse. The Falcon King sniffed the air, "I smell the bones of a human being," he cried.

"How can you imagine such a thing?" said the princess. "What human being could ever reach this city?"

"My senses have never yet deceived me. It is those brothers of yours come to look for you."

"What nonsense! hHow could they ever find their way here," replied the eldest sister. "But suppose it were my eldest brother, what would you do?"

"I would tear out his eyes with my sharp beak," cried the Falcon King.

"But suppose it were my second brother?"

"I would not only tear out his eyes but I would stew them and eat them."

"And if it were my youngest brother?"

"Ah! that would be different. Your youngest brother gave you to me in marriage and if he were to appear, I would treat him as a true friend."

"My youngest brother is here," said the princess as she flung open the door and revealed the prince.

"You are my true brother," said the Falcon King. "What can I do to help you?"

The prince told his story and asked the Falcon King to help him find Bashtchelik. "My dear brother," said the King, "I beg you to give up such an idea for it is impossible for you to succeed. In heaven and earth there is no power that can overcome Bashtchelik. Forget about the past and go home to your own country. If you will abandon this adventure I will give you a horse laden with gold."

"I cannot give it up," said the prince, "for Bashtchelik has taken away my dearly loved wife and her I cannot desert."

"If you are determined on this enterprise," said the King, "I will give you what help I can. Here is a golden feather from my wing. Whenever you are in dire need burn this feather and all the hosts of the falcons will fly to your aid."

The prince thanked the Falcon King with all his heart and the next day, saying goodbye to his dear friends, he set out once more upon his quest.

He journeyed through still more wild and desolate lands till among the mountains he came to a second city. Like the first it was deserted and he rode through empty streets. Again he heard a voice calling him and this time he turned to find his second sister, who greeted him with joy. She told him that she was the bride of the Eagle King and she led him to her tower chamber where all day long they told each other of their adventures. At night there could be heard the flight of many pinions.

"It is my husband returning," said the princess. "I must hide you for he does not love my brothers."

The Eagle King swooped into the room: "I smell the flesh of a human being!"

"You have strange ideas," said the princess. "As though a human being could make his way to these castle walls!"

"I can smell what I can smell," replied the Eagle King. "It is those worthless brothers of yours who have come to seek you."

"You are troubling yourself for nothing," said the princess. "However, suppose my elder brother did come, what would you do?"

"I would tear out his heart with my sharp beak."

"And suppose it were my second brother?"

"I would not only tear out his heart, but I would rend it into little pieces, stew them and gobble them all up."

"And what about my youngest brother?"

"Ah! that would be different. Your youngest brother was willing to give you to me in marriage, and if he were to appear I would treat him as a true friend."

The princess immediately flung open the door and revealed her youngest brother, who was received with great joy. After he had told his adventures he asked for help against Bashtchelik, but the Eagle King also tried to dissuade him, offering him two horses laden with gold if only he would return to his own country. The prince thought of his bride and was adamant.

When the Eagle King saw that the prince was determined he also gave him a golden feather from his wing.

"When you are in trouble, burn this," he said, "and I will fly to your aid with all my hosts of eagles."

The next morning the prince bade farewell and continued on his journey. His way lay through even wilder and more rocky country than before, and at last on a lofty crag overhanging a deep ravine he came upon a mountain city. Like the others it seemed to be uninhabited. But, again he heard his name called and lo and behold! it was his youngest sister. She told him that she was the wife of the Dragon King and she led him to her castle room where they spent the day together for they had much to tell. Towards evening the earth seemed to tremble. "It is my husband, the Dragon King, returning," said the princess. "I must hide you for I fear he does not love my brothers." When the Dragon King entered there was no sign of the prince, but he snorted loudly and cried, "I smell the blood of a human being."

"How can there be a human being here?" replied the princess. "You have travelled far to-day and are remembering what you smelt on your journey."

"Woman, I know what I know, it is those brothers of yours who have come to seek you."

"How could it be?" said the princess. "But supposing it were my eldest brother?"

"I would claw out his liver with my sharp talons."

"And if it were my second brother?"

"I would tear his liver into ribbons, stew every morsel until it was soft and tender and then gobble it all up."

"And if it were my youngest brother?"

"That would be completely different. He alone obeyed his Father's dying wish in allowing you to marry me. I should welcome him as a true friend."

The princess then led forward her brother and he and the Dragon King embraced with joy.

But when the prince mentioned Bashtchelik, the Dragon King also begged him to give up the search, offering him three horses laden with gold if he would go home in peace. However, when the prince would not yield he gave him a golden feather from his wing, saying, "In time of need burn this and with all my dragon hosts I will be there to give you aid."

The Dragon King told the prince that to reach the home of Bashtchelik he must cross a high range of mountains and a wide plain and beyond that lay a mighty cave which was the favorite haunt of this terrible being.

The prince continued his journey and at last, after many trials he succeeded in traversing the mountain range and crossing the wide plain until he saw the cave in the distance. There in the entrance stood his wife, her hair shining in the sunlight. The prince ran forward. "My dear, dear wife, I have found you at last. Now you can come home with me."

"But how can I?" said the princess. "Bashtchelik will find that I have gone and will pursue us."

"But you are my wife and not Bashtchelik's and if he chases us I shall fight him, for have I not four lives?"

The Princess was very much troubled, but the prince seated her on his horse and they rode away as swiftly as the horse could carry them. All day they continued on their journey until at last the sun began to set. In the evening

119

Bashtchelik returned from his travels over the world, expecting the princess to welcome him home. But the cave was empty. With a wild shriek he flew up into the air and winging his flight in ever widening circles surveyed the landscape for some sign of his captive. He gazed far into the distance but could see no movement, and soon it would be dark for the sun was already sinking behind the hills.

The prince and the princess were riding their hardest to reach the shelter of the woods, when they heard a whirring sound above them. "O merciful heaven," cried the princess, "it is Bashtchelik. Fly faster! Fly faster!"

They were already near the welcoming shadow of the trees when the last ray of the sun sent forth its light across the plain. From afar Bashtchelik saw a gleam. It was the beautiful golden hair of the princess streaming in the wind. With a cry of joy he swooped through the air. Before the prince could leap from his horse or draw his sword he found himself clasped in a firm grip.

"Foolish prince!" said Bashtchelik in sorrowful anger. "Out of gratitude I gave thee three lives. One of them is now lost. Do not tempt my anger a second time."

The prince found himself alone upon the plain. Far away, Bashtchelik was bearing the princess into captivity.

The prince was brave and did not lose heart. A second and a third time he came with swifter horses, but Bashtchelik overtook him and deprived him of two more lives.

The third time the great winged being said sternly, "O Prince, the three lives which I gave thee in gratitude are now lost and only thine own remains. It is thy last. Do not make the attempt again for no power on earth can overcome me."

The prince pondered sadly. He was quite determined not to leave his wife with Bashtchelik, but he had only one hope left and if he were not to fail again he must find some new way. Suddenly he remembered the golden feathers of the Falcon, the Eagle and the Dragon Kings. Once more he made his way to the cave, and gave the feathers to the princess.

"We will flee once more," he said, "but this time as Bashtchelik swoops above us, I will draw my sword and you must set fire to the three feathers, then the hosts of the falcons, the eagles and the dragons will come to our aid and Bashtchelik will be driven far away."

All happened as the prince had foretold.

As Bashtchelik appeared the princess set light to the feathers and the air was full of pinions. The sun darkened behind a cloud of wings and for a while nothing could be heard but the wild scream of birds. At last Bashtchelik retreated and the three kings cried out that the fight had been won. But when they turned to look at the prince he lay dead upon the ground, for Bashtchelik had struck him a death blow before turning to flee.

The Falcon, the Eagle and the Dragon Kings held counsel, and the Falcon King said, "On the slopes of a distant mountain flows the spring of the water of life."

"We will send a messenger," cried the Eagle King, "and our brother-in-law will be restored with its healing draught."

"My dragons will be the speediest couriers," proclaimed the Dragon King, "they will be there and return again within one beat of the heart."

The dragons were as good as his words: within one beat of the heart they were there and back with the water of life. The three Kings sprinkled the water over the silent form of their brother-in-law and at once he opened his eyes and looked around.

"Where is the princess?" he asked. But she was nowhere to be found, for in the general confusion, Bashtchelik had had no difficulty in carrying her away with him once more to his mountain cave.

"I must go to find her," said the prince.

"Listen!" said the three Kings. "It is useless to continue this game. No power on earth can overcome Bashtchelik unless we learn the source of his hidden strength. You must seek out the princess while Bashtchelik is away on his travels and ask her to find out from him where his strength lies. She must use her skill and her cunning to woo the knowledge from him. Then we shall know what to do."

The prince agreed. He sought the princess once more and asked her to coax the knowledge from Bashtchelik for her future freedom depended upon it. He himself would hide in the mountains and come again the next day to see if she had made the discovery.

That night when Bashtchelik returned the princess appeared very loving.

"Dear Bashtchelik," she said, "our peace together need no longer be disturbed, for thou hast shown thyself stronger and greater than any power on this earth. I love thy strength and thy grandeur. But tell me, in what does thy strength lie? I would fain bind thee with my hair to show that my love is greater than thy power."

Bashtchelik laughed. "My strength lies in my sword," he cried. "Take that away and I would be as weak and helpless as thy prince."

The princess took the sword and set it up in a corner of the cave. Then she bowed before it and began to sing a song of praise to the great powerful sword which made Bashtchelik a hero.

Bashtchelik began to laugh. "Foolish woman!" he said. "There is no power in my sword or in its scabbard."

"Thou art making mock of me," said the princess, "it was ever so, no hero will believe that his wife can honour and love him enough."

"If it is thy wish to know I will tell thee," said Bashtchelik. "My strength lies in my bow and arrows which are of magic made."

Then the princess took the bow and arrows and doing homage chanted a paean of praise to their swiftness and their death dealing power.

Bashtchelik laughed again. "Little value were my bow and arrows without the strength and skill of their master," he cried.

The princess appeared to weep. "Thou dost not love me," she said. "Thou speakest many fair words but thy deeds show that thou canst only despise me."

Bashtchelik was disturbed for he wished very much to win the love of the princess and until now she had shown no sign of affection.

"Why dost thou wish to know?" he asked.

"That I may love and honour thee the better."

"Like all women thou wilt tell it abroad."

"Whom can I tell, seeing that the prince, my husband, is dead. It is clear that thou dost not love me."

Then Bashtchelik, believing that the prince was dead, and anxious to win her love, said: "Not far from here rises a great and lofty mountain whose summit reaches to the sky and whose roots are planted deep into the earth. Within it is a cave where a serpent lies asleep. Near the serpent hides a fox. If anyone were to capture him, from his mouth would spring forth a bird, and if the bird were caught, there would leap from its beak a fish. If the fish were brought to land, from its jaws would roll an egg. In that egg lies my strength, and whoso destroys that egg, destroys me."

Then the princess folded Bashtchelik in her hair and lulled him asleep. "O Bashtchelik," she murmured, "there is indeed no one like to thee in strength."

The next day the prince came to the cave and learned the secret. He called his friends, the Falcon, the Eagle and the Dragon Kings and they consulted together. They planned that the prince should hunt out the fox and then the hosts of the falcons, the eagles and the dragons would give chase.

All happened as they had planned. The prince searched until he found the mountain whose summit reached the sky and whose roots were planted in the earth. Within the cave where the serpent lay coiled in sleep he roused the fox and drove him forth. Swift as lightning the fox darted across the plain, but swifter far was the flight of the falcon hosts. From every side they swooped upon him and clasped him in their sharp claws. From the mouth of the fox started a bird. Away, away it went through the clouds like a meteor. But still more rapid was the motion of the eagle squadrons in their chase. Now they had him in their talons.

But out of the beak of the bird leapt a fish. Down it dived into the lake and disappeared below the waters.

Now the dragons came upon the scene. Into the waves they plunged and swift was their pursuit through the swirling currents. Now their leader was upon the bank, the fish between his jaws. He laid it at the feet of the prince and from its mouth there fell an egg.

But the egg began to roll. Over the ground and down the bank towards the water it went spinning. In one moment it would be swallowed up in the deep.

The prince leapt forward. He put his foot upon the egg and crushed it. Then the Kings made a great fire and threw the egg into the flames. As the fire soared a strange sight met their eyes. Before them in the fire lay a great winged being prone and helpless.

As they gazed it changed and shrank in the searing heat until at last the flames died down, leaving only the charred wings and burnt heart. This was all that remained of the great Bashtchelik.

The prince and princess, now reunited, returned to the Czar who was overjoyed to see his daughter once more and to learn of the death of his old enemy. The eldest two princes after a long and vain search came back and heard of their youngest brother's exploits and the discovery of their sisters.

Thus all ended in happiness and there was no cloud to darken their future, for the great Bashtchelik was dead.

—*Russian Fairy Tale*

Alleluia For All Things

Of all created things, of earth and sky,
Of God and Man, things lowly and things high,
We sing this day with thankful hearts and say,
Alleluia.

Of Light and Darkness and the colors seven
Stretching their rainbow bridge from earth to heaven,
We sing this day with thankful hearts and say,
Alleluia.

Of Sun and Moon, the lamps of Night and Day,
Stars and the Planets sounding on their way,
We sing this day with thankful hearts and say,
Alleluia.

Of Times and Seasons, evening and fresh morn,
Of Birth and Death, green blade and golden corn,
We sing this day with thankful hearts and say,
Alleluia.

Of all that lives and moves, the Winds ablow,
Fire and old Ocean's never-resting flow,
We sing this day with thankful hearts and say,
Alleluia.

Of Earth and from earth's darkness springing free
The flowers outspread, the Heavenward reaching tree,
We sing this day with thankful hearts and say,
Alleluia.

Of creatures all, the eagle in his flight,
The patient ox, the lion that trusts his might,
We sing this day with thankful hearts and say,
Alleluia.

Of Man, with hand outstretched for service high,
Courage at heart, truth in his steadfast eye,
We sing this day with thankful hearts and say,
Alleluia.

Of Angels and Archangels, Spirits clear,
Warders of Souls and Watchers of the Year,
We sing this day with thankful hearts and say,
Alleluia.

Of God made Man, and through Man sacrificed,
Of Man through love made God, Adam made Christ,
We sing this day with thankful hearts and say,
Alleluia.

—*A. C. Harwood.*

Morning Prayer

To wonder at beauty
Stand guard over truth
Look up to the noble,
Resolve on the good:
This leadeth us truly
To purpose in living
To right in our doing
To peace in our feeling
To light in our thinking,
And teaches us trust
In the working of God,
In all that there is
In the width of the world
In the depth of the soul.

—*Rudolf Steiner*

To the Grown-ups

This book arose from the need of Rudolf Steiner schools for a reading book for young children from seven to nine, which could be to them a friend and companion through their early schooldays and which would open to them a door into a new kingdom. The contents are not strictly graded, but on the whole the stories and poems at the beginning are shorter and simpler and follow the course of the year from Advent and Christmas through the four seasons to the following Christmas and New Year.

We have chosen the stories and poems for their content and beauty of language, which can stimulate the imagination of the children and work upon their minds through their artistic form. They have been selected from fairy tales, fables, and legends of all nations. Some of the poems that are given in unabridged form may perhaps be found difficult, but even young children can live with their pictures and experience their artistic beauty, long before the intellect is ready to grasp their thought content.

Acknowledgments

For this book we are indebted to Caroline von Heydebrand, who in 1928 edited "Der Sonne Licht," the first reading book of the Waldorf School, Stuttgart, and to the teachers who have kindly allowed us to use any of the contents.

We also wish to thank all teachers of Rudolf Steiner schools in the U.K. who have sent contributions and given us advice and encouragement.

Permission for the use of copyright poems has kindly been given by Walter de la Mare, and Messrs. Methuen for "When Mary goes walking" by Patrick Chalmers.

—*Elisabeth Gmeyner and Joyce M. Russell*